PHILOSOPHY IN AMERICA
AN AMS REPRINT SERIES

AM I GETTING AN EDUCATION?

AMS PRESS
NEW YORK

AM I GETTING AN EDUCATION?

BY

GEORGE A. COE
JOHN DEWEY
WILLIAM LYON PHELPS
PAUL PORTER
FRANK D. SLUTZ
J. STITT WILSON
SHERWOOD EDDY

GARDEN CITY   NEW YORK
DOUBLEDAY, DORAN & COMPANY, Inc.
1929

Library of Congress Cataloging in Publication Data

Main entry under title:

Am I getting an education?

(Philosophy in America)
Reprint of the 1929 ed. published by Doubleday,
Doran, Garden City, N.Y.
CONTENTS: Coe, G. A. By-products of the college
classroom.—Phelps, W. L. How to acquire a love of
good reading.—Porter, P. A student looks at
education. [etc.]
1. Education—Addresses, essays lectures.
2. Education, Higher—Addresses, essays,
lectures. 3. United States—Intellectual life
—Addresses, essays, lectures. 4. Education—
Russia—Addresses, essays, lectures. I. Coe,
George Albert, 1862–1951.
LB7.A6 1980 370 75-3114
ISBN 0-404-59110-8

Reprinted by arrangement with
Doubleday & Co., Inc.

Reprinted from the edition of 1929, New York. Trim size and text
area of the original have been slightly altered. [original trim size:
13.1 × 19.9 cm; text area: 10.1 × 17 cm].

MANUFACTURED
IN THE UNITED STATES OF AMERICA

CONTENTS

Am I Getting An Education?

By

GEORGE A. COE

Professorship of Philosophy, Northwestern University, 1891-1909; of Religious Education and Psychology of Religion, Union Theological Seminary, 1909-1922; of Education, Teachers College, Columbia, 1922-1927.

JOHN DEWEY

Professor of Philosophy, Columbia University, New York

WILLIAM LYON PHELPS

Lampson Professor of English Literature at Yale

PAUL PORTER

Student, University of Kansas, 1928.

FRANK D. SLUTZ

Superintendent of Schools, Pueblo, Colo., 1916; Director of the Moraine Park School, Dayton, Ohio, 1917-1928; lecturer on education and advisory member of faculty of Chicago Teachers College.

J. STITT WILSON

Lecturer on Education and Social Problems

SHERWOOD EDDY

Secretary for Asia, National Council of Young Men's Christian Associations.

AM I GETTING AN EDUCATION ?

BY-PRODUCTS OF THE COLLEGE CLASSROOM

George A. Coe

There are college classrooms in which the students are eagerly seeking some worthwhile knowledge or some worthwhile skill. They are not "seeking an education"; they are not "pulling grades"; they are not being whipped or pushed into activity by professorial authority, nor wheedled into it by professorial guile; they themselves make it their "job" for the time being to master something and to know that they have mastered it.

Students who work in this spirit usually get what they go after. Of course they do! Probably they acquire less knowledge or skill than they desire, possibly less than they expect, yet enough to make the course a success from their own point of view.

But this is not all that they acquire. If we may assume—what usually is true—that the teacher in such a course employs rigorous intellectual processes in his own part of the class work, then the student acquires method as well as content or skill—method of study and of using books and authorities, method of observation or experiment, method of analysis and criticism within a given field, method of organizing and presenting material.

Command of good method is more important than any ordinary increase of knowledge or of special skill. When good method becomes a habit, it is the same thing as ability to walk alone; professors and tutors are no longer necessary; henceforth one can provide by self-criticism what at first made the teacher indispensable.

There are other by-products also. When one eagerly seeks to know anything, the initial interest is likely to lead on into new interests. For one gets out of yesterday's mental routine, and one traverses unaccustomed roads with one's eyes open. This, too, is important. If the prime function of intellectual culture is to acquire method in the use of intelligence, the function that is second in importance is the acquisition of intellectual interests.

Students who are eager to learn tend to pool their interests by raising questions, by discussion, and by comparison and reciprocal criticism of the results of reading and of private study.

5

If, in any classroom, students are mum except when they are called upon to recite, you may be sure that they are not eager to learn, but that each is looking out for some individual advantage. They miss more than they can guess. They miss both an intellectual and a social opportunity. The habit of taking the other fellow's ideas into account; the habit of changing your views without requiring either a knock-down or a surgical operation; the ability so to put your views as to make the other fellow comfortable when you differ with him or even because you do so—this, too, flows from eagerness to learn.

In a classroom like this, honesty is natural. You will find it present up to the point where some extraneous motive begins to compete with the desire to learn. Wanting to learn is *per se* honesty endeavoring to get into action; it is honor towards one's own mind, and it generates reciprocal sincerity in a group. Indeed, one who is eager to learn has a positive motive for not concealing one's ignorance and for not exaggerating one's knowledge. In the ideal classroom-procedure the student will constantly take note of what he lacks, and he will frankly seek from others help in filling the empty places. Therefore he will welcome tests that help him to this self-knowledge. If, then, tests bring temptations to dishonesty, it is because of some factor in them other than the factor of teaching and learning.

To sum up what has been said: Granted eagerness to learn on the part of students, and reasonable competency in the teacher, these by-products appear: (1) Growth in method of intellectual work; (2) Increasing range of intellectual interests; (3) Ability to exchange ideas with others and thereby to grow intellectually and to promote growth in others; (4) Increasing ability to make social adjustments both because one learns how to understand others, and because one learns how to make changes in one's self; (5) A habit, at least within this area, of frankness and genuineness, and a willingness to be tested upon the basis of actual achievement.

Why are there so few college classrooms that correspond to this description? In order to be perfectly fair to the colleges, one must acknowledge that most freshmen bring bad habits of study and of classroom practice from their elementary and secondary schools. The college has the problem not merely of the ideal way to teach college subjects, but also the problem of what to do with unfortunate by-products of our school system. It would be well, then, for any student to ask himself these questions: Did I have good intellectual habits when I entered my college? Whether I did or not, to what extent is my present experience confirming or creating good habits and overcoming bad ones? And am I moving towards genuine intellectual maturity?

One cannot effectively face this personal issue unless one is willing to examine the particular forces that play upon one's personality in the classroom. What motives are called into action? What choices does one make? What kind of ability to get results is being acquired by getting results here and now? What intellectual interests are active, and what ones are springing up? What attitudes towards others are habitual, and what practice in social adjustment is one getting? Above all, why do these things occur?

It would not be fair to fix upon the students themselves the chief or primary blame for the present lack of intellectual interests and the present wretched methods of study and of classroom practice. For these are outstanding facts:

1. A considerable proportion of college teachers, probably a considerable majority, assume that their job consists, not in awakening intellectual interests, not even in feeding interests already here, but in getting a rigidly determined batch of material far enough inside the student's mind to enable him to reproduce it in tests and examinations. One would not believe without compelling evidence that it is common to restrict classroom converse to the contents of a text-book or of the teacher's lectures; that the reproduction of these contents determines a student's standing and recognition as a scholar; that teachers do not welcome doubt or dissent; or that eagerness to know something not contained in text-book or lectures is frustrated by the time-consuming demands of this pre-determined material. I say that one would not believe this without compelling evidence, but students in remarkable numbers have been asserting just this and complaining about it for years and years.

2. A dominant classroom force is the marking system. Theoretically it is a means of ascertaining and recording certain facts; practically it is a system of motivation. College experience does many things that are not "denominated in the bond," but the one thing that, with few exceptions, is "denominated in the bond" is the official equating of college education with getting credits towards a diploma. And this pound of flesh is exacted. It is the thing that makes students work even though they don't want to learn, and if they do want to learn it injects a second motive. Only the extraordinarily reckless chap, or the one with extraordinary intellectual independence comes anywhere near forgetting the hand that holds the whip.

Anyone who knows "the inside of the cup" can tell what the results are. First, the student avoids revealing his ignorance. He feels that he cannot afford to display the vacant places, even though displaying them be a condition of having them filled. The constant demand of the marking system is that he should make a show of what he knows, or at least remembers, not what he still lacks. Thus arises *a desire to appear to know.* It is not invented by the students, and they must not be held wholly responsible for the consequences; it is the omnipresent drive of the officially invented and maintained system.

How tricky is the desire to *appear* to know! "I crammed most of the night, using strong coffee to keep me awake. The next day I passed the examination, but on the day after the examination I knew scarcely anything about the subject"—so said a diploma holder. But the professor was satisfied; his standard had been fully met, and the degree of bachelor was in this wise fully earned in the official sense of "earning." Students acquire great skill in meeting the official requirements with economy of labor, and the means and methods of doing it are handed down by each campus generation to its successor.

This is tricky beyond all that the students understand it to be, for it tricks the students themselves, not merely the professors. One learns most, as a rule, at the point where one is most intently and purposefully active. In this case, the chief learning is "how to get by," and what is learned from the text-book becomes, psychologically considered, a by-product!

Outright dishonesty in tests follows, of course; for the system invites and rewards it. More than this, the system provides the means and the process whereby initial honor, if it be there, is gradually undermined. For concealment of one's ignorance and making a show of what one knows or remembers meets the professor upon his own ground upon his own terms. At the same time this ground and these terms are unavowed or denied. Theoretically the aim of a course of instruction is mastery of a body of material and of the methods appropriate thereto, but in prac-tice this is not the aim of either professor or student, for both of them head straight for grades determined by specific types of test. There is therefore an inherent and systemic, though unintended, insincerity all 'round, and this insincerity greases the incline that begins with concealment and ends with complete falsehood.

Cribbing, accordingly, is the joint product of professor and student—rather, since the professor is under pressure to work a preëstablished system, it is the joint product of the student and the college as a teaching entity. College officers who think they are engaged in education support and prolong a system that produces concealment, evasion and lying.

3. The introduction of "objective tests" (the right-wrong, multiple choice and completion tests) is creating problems as well as solving problems. The intention is to reduce the errors that inhere in any system that grades students upon the sole basis of a teacher's judgment. This brings relief to the teacher, and the results are, in a sense, fairer to the student. But "objective

tests" are as yet a part of the marking system, and this is a system of motivation. What effect, then, do these new tests, in this setting, have upon students' attitudes and methods of study?

Conversation with students in two or three colleges has yielded an unambiguous reply. A student of high native ability and class standing, one who has intellectual interests and enjoys studying, said: "When I know that one of these objective tests is to be given, I change my method of preparation. I go over the entire text, studying the words one by one so that I cannot get caught upon any of them." "But surely," I questioned, "if you know the structure of the subject, and the evidence for all the important conclusions, this is enough?" "Not at all," he answered, "I could know all that and yet not pass." Other students declared—and as yet I have found no contrary instance—that their methods of study have become more mechanical. To the extent that this is the effect of these new methods of testing, they are fostering the "get by" motive, defeating the ends of scholarship, and hindering the formation of sound character.

4. Notice, next, the overwhelming prominence of the professor or instructor in the classroom. The lecture method is not the only form of it. In multitudes of instances in which this method is not used the students sit, like a patient in a dentist's chair, waiting silently to have something done to them; and the teacher accepts this relationship! Students "speak when they are spoken to," and the less often they are spoken to the luckier they think they are. If a student asks a question, or volunteers information, he is in danger, in some colleges, of falling under the suspicion of wanting to curry favor with the teacher. There is many a classroom in which free intellectual give-and-take between teacher and student rarely occurs. The relation between the two is strictly official, and it tends to become mechanical. In college after college, students express a longing to get really acquainted with members of the faculty, and the assumption appears to be common that really knowing a professor as a person depends altogether upon contacts outside the classroom. That is, the learned man, as such, is an aloof individual; his learning is not one of the warm bonds, as it might be, between himself and the learner. This situation, like the others already mentioned, is not a creation of students; it is the official approach of the college to her so-called sons and daughters.

5. Under the four conditions that have been described, there grows up, in the nature of the case, antagonism on the part of students towards faculties. It is different, in one respect at least, from the antagonism that was rife two generations ago. For it grows in only minor degree out of systems of discipline. In former days there was continuous hostility because the faculty

made, and endeavored to enforce by penalties and sometimes by espionage, rules of conduct that the students didn't want to obey—often, of course, because they objected to dictation rather than to the standards in question. With the decay of this old, self-defeating discipline, we have seen much of the old hostility disappear; but there remains, and perhaps it is growing, a kind of tension that may be still worse. For it is *resistance to the teaching function of the college as it is understood by both faculty and students.* The nature of it was clearly indicated a few months ago by remarks attributed to the president of a large university. He is reported to have expressed the opinion that the time had about come when colleges should stop trying to educate students who do not want to be educated.

This hostility reaches through a long scale of particular facts. At one end of the scale we find a conviction on the part of some students that this or that teacher does not, and will not, meet students half way upon any matter that concerns his acts as teacher. "If I question any view that he presents in the classroom, he will mark me down"; "If we question the fairness of an examination or of his grading, he will 'have it in for us'"; "When a man gives as unfair an examination as M. N. did, I hold that cribbing is justifiable"—such are the remarks that one hears. Of course these students are often mistaken as to professorial attitudes. "I went to him quaking," said one student, "but he received me most cordially, and I came away ashamed of my distrust of him." But, whether teachers are misjudged or not, the significant fact remains that something is producing distrust.

This at one end of the scale; at the other end an unemotional attitude of wary watchfulness of all faculty moves, grudging compliance with requirements, avoidance of the appearance of coöperation, a turning to unintellectual affairs for "real living," and scorn for any "student" who finds his chief delight in study. It is easy to find college communities in which these sentiments are so general that earnest students who are pleased with their opportunities conceal the fact. To get "kick" out of classroom work is not in good form.

The causes of this set of attitudes are complex. A professor asked: "Hasn't the spirit of the non-academic world about us overflowed the college walls and overwhelmed us?" Undoubtedly, for students come, in increasing proportion, from homes that lack academic traditions, and meantime modern young men and women have wider contacts with the world, and unprecedented means and instruments for varied enjoyable activities. But after all this has been acknowledged, we must come back to the question whether intellectual aims and exertions are inevitably irksome to young people. If so, the faculties, when they meet suspicion and resistance, are simply fulfilling their doom; if not, then the faculties should so modify their practices as to reveal the joys of the intellectual life, and to awaken eagerness to learn.

These five sets of facts do not, of course, give us a balanced account of American academic life. No one knows how far the cancer has spread, nor what the "average" college experience is like. Many students, in the aggregate, experience an intellectual awakening, and many acquire valuable preparation for scientific, literary, or other careers. But these successes of the colleges are attained at the cost of enormous human waste. The facts just recited are sufficiently frequent to require the assumption that every student who enters college enters perils to his intellectual life and through it to his general integrity.

It is encouraging that professors and administrators are giving increasing attention to this fact of waste, and that they are experimenting with several schemes for reducing it. I shall not add to the already considerable material descriptive of these schemes; instead, I shall confine the remainder of my remarks to the question, What can students themselves do to improve the classroom situation?

To advise students to "study harder" is easy, and it is nearly futile. For the methods of "study" are vicious, and the officially approved processes of "teaching" stand in the way. What is needed in this situation is that students, instead of reluctantly submitting to self-defeating teaching, should actively work for reform of it.

Upon several campuses a desire is already becoming articulate for education as distinguished from grades, diplomas, and the honors of so-called "scholarship." What is still more striking is the amount of investigative thinking that undergraduates are doing concerning the nature and the processes of real education. Student journals, student committees, and student conventions and conferences bear witness to this fact. Moreover—and this should be placed alongside the five sets of disquieting facts—college authorities are taking much of the student criticism as coöperation, and they are asking for more of it. Indeed, there is danger that the hospitality that student reformers receive will lead them to think that their task is less difficult and drastic than it is.

Students, like their elders, over-simplify problems, and then expect too much from this or that particular reform-mechanism. They jump into honor systems as a cure for cribbing, but honor systems fail to cure; for the college, by its official methods of teaching, testing, marking and graduating, constantly trains new recruits to habits of evasion and pretence. Jumping back to the system of proctors will not even check this infection. "Honors courses" for juniors and seniors who have won high grades in freshman and sophomore work seem—wonderful to relate—like an almost revolutionary advance. But what is the significance of high freshman and sophomore grades? What about the other juniors and seniors and all the underclassmen? If a really creative principle has been discovered, its validity can hardly be restricted to any superior group, certainly not to superiority determined by existing freshman and sophomore tests. More "cuts," more electives, fewer lecture courses, less dependence upon reproductive memory, courses that are more closely related to current problems, general revision of the curriculum? Perhaps; but from each of these, however sound it may be in itself, too much will be expected. The reason is that, whereas the basic difficulty in all the sombre facts that I have detailed is one of motives and purposes, these reforms do not sufficiently provide for any new dynamic of the mind.

The student may as well make up his mind that education is not something that an institution does to him or bestows upon him. His professors haven't it in their keeping, and he cannot acquire it by accommodating himself to them. The way out of the present peril is for the student to commune with himself as to what he really wants, and then to go implacably after it!

Not less, but more, should the professor ask the same question from his own station. For he, because of more deeply ingrained mental habits, is even more likely than the student to rest his mind upon the pillow of comfortable general terms. Few teachers have had a college training that equips them to understand the dynamics of their own minds and of the minds about them; few of them realize that teaching is fundamentally a relating of the motives of the teacher to the motives of the learner in such a way that the learner's motives grow. Hence the paradox of professors who devotedly labor to promote culture and scholarship, but hinder both by this very devotion.

When students, shaking themselves loose from catchwords and academic conventionalities, and teachers, facing the by-products of their classrooms, get together and talk over what they respectively want, then something significant will happen. No doubt several of the schemes just mentioned will be adopted, but these will be minor happenings. Far more important will be the differentiation of students who want to learn from those who do not. Present timid minorities of intellectually eager and critical collegians will come into the open, grow in number and in courage, and at last become the academic type, while those incorrigibly indisposed to learn will be given leave to withdraw. Still more important will be the reconstruction of the whole teaching-testing-grading-graduating machine. The details of this reconstruction will be determined by the conditions already described, but it will

proceed in its totality from the simple and sensible, though revolutionary, assumption that students desire to learn.

When this assumption prevails, it will be evident that the teacher's first duty is to induce the student to judge this desire critically. What do I want to know? Why just this rather than something else? Can I learn this without first learning something else? What tools must I be able to command? What processes are essential? What is the evidence of success or failure? The professor who works with the student in the sphere of such self-propulsion will not fail of the influence that his wider experience justifies. In fact, the danger always will be that the awakened student will lean too heavily upon his more learned friend.

The marking system, with its intrusion of artificial and corrupting motives, will disappear, but tests will not. They will be more thorough rather than less, for they will seek evidence of independent power and productiveness, not (as at present) of dependent reproductiveness. Whether we shall have "graduating classes" (with their apparently inevitable tendency towards cheap standardization) is doubtful, but we need have no doubt that genuine productivity or concrete evidence that the student can use his intellect to advantage will receive recognition.

One can imagine "commencement day" transformed into an exhibit of student productions expressive of student interests and desires, productions as varied as the personalities represented. One will be represented by a literary essay; another by a poem; another by a piece of historical or scientific or philosophical learning that he himself has dug out; a musical composition will speak for one, a mechanical invention for another, and skill in the manipulation of important processes will be duly registered.

In some such direction lies the imperative reform of college education. There are signs that it is starting, and that the present generation of undergraduates can have a part in it if they so desire.

HOW TO ACQUIRE A LOVE OF GOOD READING
WHILE IN COLLEGE

By WILLIAM LYON PHELPS

The best time to acquire a love of good reading, along with many other good habits, is long before one enters college. It never disturbs me to see small boys absorbed in detective and adventure stories; because I know that through this ephemeral trash they have found something of the magic of books. They have learned that at any moment they can be transported from the world of reality into a fairyland, and thus they have for the rest of their lives ready access to a source of enjoyment that will serve them as a refuge from many of the cares and troubles of life, and may also keep them from other recreations that have no merit at all. Furthermore, if a boy or girl really loves reading, literary taste can be cultivated, and better books will take the place of cheap ones; whereas, if there is no love of reading at all, it is very difficult to arouse interest in books after one has grown up without them.

I divide all readers into two classes—those who read to *remember,* and those who read to *forget.* I consider that one of my chief duties as a professional teacher is to persuade members of the second group to enter the first. Of course there are times when the most serious men and women must read to forget. But those times are emergencies, or at best times of recreation. The immense pleasure of reading, for ambitious and seriously-minded people, is enormously increased when the reading not only entertains, but also inspires and develops the mind, while adding to one's stock of facts and ideas.

There are many young men and women who are not intellectually awakened until they enter a university; and I have known more than a few who are not thus aroused until the last two years of their college course. It may be that some particular subject or some particular instructor makes an especial appeal to their imagination; and while it is better if a student enters college with a good intellectual background, for many circumstances have made this impossible, and, after all, it is never too late to make a start.

Champion Gene Tunney, in an address on Shakespeare that he delivered before my class in literature at Yale, said something that is universally applicable. He said that although his listeners had had every advantage and he had had none, if they really wished to master a subject, they would have to do exactly what he had done, that is, they would have to do the work themselves. Teachers may give information and perhaps inspiration, but they cannot do the work for their pupils. The pupils must acquire knowledge by their own efforts.

One of the greatest faults in American college education is that so few students seem to have the power of initiative. They do more or less what they are told to do, learn their assigned lessons, and fulfill the requirements for a degree. But what they ought to do is to read all around a favorite subject, and work it up for themselves. No one should feel that he has successfully completed a college course if he has merely taken the required number of units, and passed the required number of examinations. No one should leave college without having acquired a love of good reading, a love so sincere and intense that good reading will become a life habit. This is the real reason why graduation is called *Commencement*. It should be the beginning of a life of culture.

An enormous amount of time is wasted in college. The first thing a student should do is to organize his leisure. There must be room for athletics, social engagements, and good conversation with his college mates. But all this still leaves time for good reading. I do not wish to hold myself up as an example, but I cite my own case merely to prove that I am not suggesting a course for others to follow that I have not myself found practicable. In my Freshman year at Yale, we had an excellent instructor in Greek, Horatio M. Reynolds. I remember very well his telling the class one day that they should not be content merely to learn the assigned lesson, but that they ought to read Greek history by and for themselves. This seemed to me desirable, and I set apart one hour every day during which in the solitude of my dormitory room I read Grote's History of Greece. I had a happy time as an undergraduate, but some of my happiest hours were spent not in athletics and in social pleasures, though I keenly enjoyed those things; they were spent alone, reading Greek history. The result was that I became deeply interested in Greek and in ancient history, and it has interested me all my life.

The love of good reading grows by what it feeds on; if one reads the best authors outside of the classroom, one's appetite for good books steadily increases. A very good thing is to buy a few books, as one learns to love them. It is a mistake to buy sets of books all at once; they look well on the shelves, but one does not read them. Buy an individual book, and master it.

Then each book is an inspiring personality, a tried and good friend.

There is not the slightest doubt in my mind that the majority of students waste too much time in going to the movies, and in reading the cheap popular magazines. The movies and the magazines are too often the enemies of culture, for they take up time that might more profitably be spent on good books.

Why not start with one good author, like Dickens, and read half a dozen of his best novels, say David Copperfield, Great Expectations, Bleak House, Our Mutual Friend, Pickwick Papers, and Old Curiosity Shop? Or, if one prefers tales of adventure, why not read Stevenson instead of trash? Stevenson's Treasure Island and The Ebb Tide are just as exciting as a cheap thriller, and are at the same time great works of literary art. The same is true of the love of poetry. One might begin by reading narrative poetry, like that of Scott and of John Masefield; and then read Keats's Eve of St. Agnes; then proceed to the pure poetry of Keats's Odes, and the lyrical works of Browning.

A good taste for biography, once formed, is an inestimable blessing. Boswell's Life of Johnson is the greatest of all biographies, because the people in its pages actually live in the reader's mind, and we know them better than our next-door neighbors. In American history, Franklin's Autobiography, Sandburg's Life of Lincoln, Lord Charnwood's Life of Lincoln, are three admirable books. And for the life and customs of our own day, a book that is full of both information and inspiration is The Americanization of Edward Bok, to which should be added Michael Pupin's noble work, From Immigrant to Inventor.

If a student makes up his mind that he will not graduate from college in ignorance of the best life and thought of the world, he will perhaps begin to read good books from a stern sense of duty. But duty will soon give way to pleasure, and the time will come when he would rather spend an evening with his favorite author than spend it in merely frivolous amusement. As Dean Inge says of the religious life, what begins as an experiment ends in an experience.

A STUDENT LOOKS AT EDUCATION

Paul Porter [1]

It is a commonplace that few students today go to college for a liberal education. Most matriculants are probably actuated by two incentives: (1) the desire for high social and economic position, for which a college degree is increasingly a prerequisite, and (2) the desire for the romance of college life as glorified in the novels, movies, sport pages, and popular traditions of the day. The values of four years in academic halls are inevitably judged by the degree of achievement of these two aims by those who seek them. Students, faculty and the public alike may pay lip-service to the cultivation of habits of critical thought, but this is not a major characteristic of most colleges. A minimum of intellectual activity is quite generally looked upon as an irksome but necessary means for the achievement of the first objective; it may be, and usually is, entirely divorced from the second. Rarely, indeed, is it engaged in for its own sake.

In so far as this is the prevailing campus attitude, the college is at an obvious handicap in even instilling a desire for, much less giving, a liberal education to students who are seeking merely a delightful time, a degree, or at the most, technical or professional training. Nevertheless, to justify the students' four-year leave of absence from the active world, and the expenditure of millions of dollars, we must demand that the colleges achieve their expected function of educating. Should we, upon examination, find that they are not doing so, we must look for corrective measures, and possibly toward a general reconstruction of an ailing academic order.

Our examination begins with two questions, questions incidentally, which an increasing number of critically minded students are today asking: "What are the marks of a liberally educated man or woman?" and "Are they being acquired in college?" The writer realizes that the true marks of an education are difficult to assess on paper, for an education, educators agree, is never

[1] Student of the University of Kansas, 1928, editor *University Daily Kansan*, the *Dove*, the *Cosmopolitan Student*, contributing editor to the *New Student*, college debater, president University Y. M. C. A.

wholly achieved, least of all with the receipt of a college degree; rather, it is progressive and continual adaptation to new social situations. But of many attempts at definition, the writer prefers this one of John Herman Randall, Jr., the author of the "Making of the Modern Mind":[1]

"A liberal education should place in our hands the best intellectual techniques that have been devised for the understanding of ourselves and our world, and for intelligent participation in the joint enterprise of making the most of our resources, natural and human. There are courses of training that aim to fit men to take part in the life about them in some particular niche. A liberal education should aim, not so much to fit us to take our places in our present world—God forbid!—as to provide us with the instruments to remake our world into something better. The greatest tribute to the success of the American college is that it so often sends forth its graduates intensely dissatisfied with what they have received, and unwilling to settle down in business or the professions. Its greatest failure is that it so often has provided them with no effective tools for the reconstruction of the life to which they will not, fortunately, adjust themselves."

To this may be added one further achievement that we might reasonably expect—implied, but not explicit in the foregoing—the development of a well-integrated, cultured personality on the part of the student.

Does the college equip its students with this sort of an education? Let us examine the results. On the credit side we may safely assume that a four-year college training has prepared the students for a respected place in society. It has practically guaranteed for most of them an income and a standard of living considerably above that of the average man. It has given them some understanding of themselves, and the world in which they live. Some have acquired an appreciation of literature, music and art. Probably students are more tolerant, more open-minded, more humanely sympathetic than the ordinary "man of the street." Even more valuable than these assets, they are able to continue the process of education throughout life.

But we should ask more of college than this. After all, this has only prepared them for established niches in a world which refuses to remain established. And even the niches—high as they may be—are not all that could be desired. The college must be further tested on its record of instilling in students the desire for a more intelligently and more humanely ordered world, and equipping them with the effective tools for work toward that end.

An indispensable tool is intellectual vigor. Yet, intellectual apathy, not vigor, seems to characterize most undergraduate life. The majority of the students pursue a policy of "getting by," perhaps vaguely dissatisfied with a curriculum that bores more

[1] "Science and the Educated Man." *The New Student,* Vol. 7, No. 34 (May 23, 1928).

than it stimulates, but good-naturedly accepting it as inevitable. Scant interest is evinced in current social and political issues. Few stimulating or critical books and magazines are read; intellectual topics are not the substance of the students' conversation. Mr. Robert Cooley Angell observes:[1]

"In the main there seems to be little desire for a broader and deeper understanding of life. The American undergraduate does not revel in the discovery of truth; rather the use of his mental faculties is regarded as a more or less distasteful but necessary means to the coveted ends of high social position and pecuniary gains. . . . The general run of undergraduates merely share vicariously in the traditional spirit of learning."

If such is the case, we need hardly expect an unusual display of independence of thought, which is another essential tool of the well-educated man. As a group they are freed from some of the popular opinions of the day; to a considerable extent they maintain, as do nearly all our youth, a fresh outlook upon life. But within the group a fairly strict conformity is adhered to. In some instances, unorthodox views, say, in regard to athletics are viewed as downright disloyal—a striking parallel of a tendency upon the part of some groups and individuals in the nation to represent divergent opinion as unpatriotic and traitorous. For the most part, however, opinions fail to stir them one way or the other. They are, as a professor of English literature has called his students, "damnably complacent." Well satisfied with the world as it is, they do not wander far from the mores and prejudices of their primary groups. "Revolt against the status quo?" ironically asks another professor, "They've never heard of it."

Yet these criticisms of the college are trifling compared to its failure to effect a unifying correlation between academic learning and day-by-day behavior, even on the part of those students who industriously acquire fact upon fact. Theory is one thing; practice, another. "The passionless pursuit of passionless intelligence" is the way Jack London once characterized academic life.[2]

To the extent that they are aware of the existence of certain social maladjustments, such as conflicts between races, economic classes, and nations, all too many students accept them as unwanted but necessary evils. They are deficient, frankly speaking, in the intellectual tools for coping with some of the major problems of the day. They have been taught history—history as a subject consisting of dates, of political intrigues and wars. But they haven't understood history as a grippingly fascinating and meaningful story of human progress, nor have they understood

[1] In an excellent sociological study of university undergraduate life, *The Campus,* p. 4, D. Appleton & Co., 1928.
[2] Quoted in *Twenty Years of Social Pioneering,* p. 9. League for Industrial Democracy, N. Y., 1926.

the vast social, economic and geographic forces involved. They have been taught ethics—ethics as a dry mass of abstract absolutes. Not ethics as progressive, pragmatic and relative norms of human conduct, involved in every circumstance and act of the group, as well as the individual! They have studied science. They can dissect a frog in the laboratory, and name the principal parts of its anatomy. But their approach to human problems is far from scientific. They have failed to carry over into daily life-situations the precision, the patience, the scrupulous objective examination of every detail and circumstance, that characterized their laboratory investigations.

Surely the scientific spirit is a necessary intellectual tool for an adequate understanding of life! Surely a historical understanding is an indispensable instrument in mastering the great social forces of the age! Surely the ethics which we have culled from human experience must guide our experience to come—the conduct of national, economic, racial and religious groups, as well as the conduct of individuals!

Yet, the life equipment of the average student or graduate includes these tools only in crude and rudimentary form. College has given them tools—no one would deny this—but not sharp tools, not penetrating tools. Tools that only scratch the surface, that make for superficiality, that can only give a new veneer to old habits. A veneer of automobiles and radios and plumbing over medieval attitudes! Not tools that make for a reconstruction of a social order that will rely upon science and human understanding, rather than chance and supernaturalism!

II.

Sweeping criticism of the educational system, however, does not solve the problem of reconstructing it to fit recognized needs. We have witnessed in the post-war years a period of facile revolt on the part of the more critically minded youth against the academic order, in toto. Even college presidents, in any number of magazine articles, have been scarcely less discriminating in apportioning all blame to inadequate preparation of the students for the sort of education the college offered; or to students' distraction by athletics, and the external and specious.

"The side shows are so numerous, so diverting—so important if you will —that they have swallowed up the circus, and those who perform in the main tent must often whistle for their audience, discouraged and humiliated," [1]

complained Woodrow Wilson as President of Princeton. Yet the net result of this criticism has been little more than the emphasizing

[1] "What Is College For?" *Scribner's,* XLVI (1909) p. 576.

of the fact that modern education is essentially bankrupt. Our next step must be to isolate and analyze the factors that make for an ailing system, and then consider specific remedies for them. In doing this, we will find, I believe, that students, teachers, those who control the college, and the society in which it is rooted, all contribute to its bankruptcy.

In the first place, many students are not prepared for the type of education we have envisioned, even if they enrolled in college seeking it. Their high school training is conducive to anything but independence of mind and resourcefulness. High school teaching is generally rote teaching—mental regimentation and drill. Moreover, most students come from middle-class families who have no strong cultural tradition, and who are eminently satisfied with the world as it is. Their contact with the world has been restricted to certain well-sheltered spheres, and their knowledge of the social problems facing this generation are, therefore, generally meagre and vicarious. Mr. Angell [1] believes that if a greater proportion of students were drawn from the families of culture, which are comparatively few, or were drawn from working-class families, their interest in learning would be more vital and sincere. This is probably true, but we must for the present concern ourselves with the material at hand. Granted inadequate background and preparation on the part of the students, the college must set itself to the tremendous task of overcoming these handicaps.

The method of teaching, it seems to me, is frequently a real barrier to education. An outworn concept of learning prevails in many a classroom, even unconsciously with professors who consciously deny its validity. I refer to the theory that students are in college to be instructed. On the basis of this false conception of education, professors reel off yards and yards of facts—information in the bulk, to be jotted down in notebooks and assimilated, and later reported back to the professors in examinations. "Fifty-minute doses of wisdom," [2] is the way one student satirized his classes. And then these teachers bemoan the fact that students do not think for themselves! Under present conditions can we expect them to do so? As modern psychologists have pointed out, independent and creative thinking is a habit, and can be cultivated only through the repeated experience of self-reliance. What students need is not blue prints of the paths to knowledge painstakingly charted for them, but instead the experience of making their own explorations and their own discoveries, with the assistance of the teacher, of

[1] Robert Cooley Angell, *The Campus*, p. 34.
[2] *The Dove*, Vol. I, No. 3. (University of Kansas.)

course, as guide and counsellor, but never captain. If fewer teachers taught, and more of them simply opened new vistas of thought, and then challenged the students to make their own explorations, it is reasonable to believe that fewer students would be conventional drifters, and more of them would be creative leaders in world affairs.

Drawing generalization about the capability of the faculty, I realize, is treading on risky ground, but I believe I may safely say that no small number of teachers are, to varying degrees, hindering true education. They have not the ability to interest their students, far less inspire. Their teaching is mechanical, pedantic, and depersonalized—just so much grist from a mill. They can dissect knowledge into dead, unrelated bits, but their aloofness from the active world makes it impossible for them to give their learning meaning or force in actual life situations. Fortunately this type of professor seems to be decreasing in number. Most teachers are independent and resourceful, in certain areas of their conduct, at least. They manifest both skill and imagination in gaining a mastery of whatever branch of knowledge happens to be their specialty, and in relating that branch to the whole.

Yet, despite these qualities, they may be lacking in one essential that would make them the most desirable leaders of youth— and that is the experience of sharing in the control of their own most vital affairs. It is difficult for anyone, even college professors, to teach someone else the art of democratic self-government, when they, themselves, are inexperienced in that field. Unfortunately, the teachers have been deplorably weak when engaged in the joint enterprise of meeting the problems of their profession.

Under the present system of absentee control of the college there is not much hope for immediate improvement. Administrative affairs are anything but democratically handled. And this is a difficulty that bears on every factor in the reconstruction of higher education, for it is a problem that cannot be disassociated from many of the major problems of today. College, however aloof from the active world it may seem to the dissatisfied sophomore, is inextricably a part of it. The same forces that have influenced the development of our present industrial civilization, have influenced the development of higher education. It has been truthfully said that college is as much an essential part of this age as is the production of automobiles. And it is a significant fact that the weaknesses, as well the benefits, of the existing order are mirrored in the educational system. The intelligent student or professor seeking democracy in our industrial and political life must face the lack of democracy on the campus.

Economists like W. Z. Ripley[1] are pointing out that industrial control is more and more being absorbed by financiers—absentee directors, if you please. Educators like Dr. J. E. Kirkpatrick[2] are pointing out that the control of education follows a similar course—if not directly into the hands of the financiers, at least into the hands of men far removed from the problems confronted by students and faculty. Whether their trusteeship is industry or higher education, the boards of directors must hire a skilled general manager to execute their policies; and the chief difference between the two types of business is that the college agent is distinguished by the title "President." The president is responsible to the faculty and students in a moral sense only, and no matter how liberal or democratic in spirit he may be, his attitude is necessarily tempered by his relationship to the board. Needless to say, not all college presidents are liberals or democrats—far from it! The professional status of the professor under such conditions is not that of a free man, guiding his own affairs in democratic coöperation with his fellows, but rather the status of the unorganized factory worker. As a department head he may become a trifle more influential; and if perchance he is a dean, he enjoys a rank comparable to division superintendent. But inevitably the system is autocratic.

The men who comprise the boards of trustees or regents are usually industrialists, financiers, or their attorneys, or their editors—at least men who represent the prevailing capitalistic point of view. Quite naturally so. With a possible few exceptions,[3] there has been no sinister conspiracy on their part to gain control of education, for control has come to them for very natural reasons: they hold the pursestrings for new buildings, new endowments, and new chairs of research; they are the most respected members of the community; and usually they are the only laymen who have the possible leisure to devote to even a casual consideration of academic affairs. Inevitably they see the problems of education through the same set of glasses that they use in their daily business. Should it be proposed to them, as occasionally it has been, that the faculty or the students, as organized bodies, should be represented on the controlling board, they would no doubt laugh at the absurdity of such an idea, as they have in the past. The proposal is as ridiculous as the thought that a hub-cap tightener might vote and par-

---

[1] *Main Street and Wall Street*, Little, Brown & Co., Boston, 1927.
[2] *The American College and Its Rulers*, New Republic, N. Y., 1926.
[3] See *The Goose Step*, by Upton Sinclair, Pasadena, Calif., 1922.

ticipate in the councils of the General Motors Corporation! Nor is it seriously considered that the faculty, much less the students, should choose their own president. But why not? Suppose the faculty, as a body, is *not* prepared to assume administrative responsibility, say in coöperation with a board representing the state, the alumni, or the public, whose fault is it that they are not prepared? And how can we logically expect them to train students in responsibility and leadership, unless they, themselves, gain practical experience in these lines?

The student, young or old, who attempts to deal with this problem, must eventually realize that democracy in education cannot be isolated from democracy in industry, or democracy in any phase of life. There can be no general reconstruction of the academic order until there is a general reconstruction in the whole social order in which it is rooted. Not until democracy is a habit, and not merely a shibboleth, of life, will it prevail on the campus. A chip from the old block is college, and the grain of the wood is the same. In this age of mass production, I think no one need be surprised that the production virus has surged through educational veins—that credit hours, quantitatively measured, rather than internal growth, is the criterion for the standardized bachelor's label; that a professor's worth is gauged by the number of "research" articles he can produce in a given time, rather than by his ability to lead and inspire students; that the fame of the college is known by the success of its athletic teams, by its grist of "Doctors of Philosophy," or by the honorary degrees it confers. A civilization that places property values above human values, and measures its own worth by the number of automobiles per family, is not the type of civilization to produce colleges and universities in which the students learn critical self-evaluation, or acquire the instruments of cultural maturity.

A realistic facing of the facts brings obvious evidence that the habits of society will not change overnight, or even within a generation. But our educational system, enjoying a function possessed by no other social institution, that of explorer and pathfinder in the vanguard of social progress, can ill afford to lag at the tail-end of the procession, and put a fatalistic faith in natural evolution for guidance. If we are to have a more intelligent, and a more humane civilization, higher education must consciously work toward that end—and progress must begin at home! Otherwise, when the promised land is reached, the college, like Moses, may find itself too weak and decrepit to enter.

III.

Suppose teaching was understood to be the stimulation of students to a critical examination of the values of our civilization. Suppose students began their climb to wisdom with an objective consideration of their own problems—problems that they will meet throughout life—and then expanded their horizons through (1) intimate contacts with representatives of diverse races, creeds, and classes, (2) a browsing among the recorded experiences of the past, (3) intimate chats with men of wisdom and broad experience, who could vivify the past, and give it meaning for the present. Suppose the method was that of cooperative shared experience in which students and teacher sat down together and just talked things over. Would this promote the kind of a liberal education we are seeking? I believe it would.

If we interpret the word "educate" according to what its Latin derivative seems to imply—"lead out"—we will understand the academic process as leading students out of provincialism, out of their narrow spheres and their limited areas of contact, into a wide world of cosmopolitanism. The writer, in reflecting upon his own experience, sees four things that he believes have contributed as much to his intellectual development as all the academic formalism of writing theses, auditing lectures, and cramming facts. These were: (1) two summers spent in industrial work, during which time he frequently met with a small group of other workers in various industries for an informal, even jovial, sharing of experiences; (2) various intercollegiate conferences in which students, professors, and non-academic leaders discussed democratically their most vital interests; (3) four semesters of living in a Cosmopolitan house with students from many nations; and (4) a three-months study trip to the Orient, made in company with a small party of other students, under the leadership of a man who was not only an eminent authority on the social and political life, the history, and the culture of the lands visited, but who had the dynamic enthusiasm to give his knowledge meaning and vitality.

These informal, but none the less valuable methods of education, I believe, deserve a more prominent place in our educational system. I propose, then, the following steps in the reconstruction of the academic order—steps to be followed not as a fixed program, but as flexible ultimate aims, adaptable to such widely divergent conditions as may exist, say, between Yale and a small Nebraska denominational college:

1. *Expanded horizons for the students.* Students who have been sheltered from the hardships of an industrial society might

well be encouraged to study economics and sociology by the "case" method. Let them, as elective work toward a degree, spend a semester or two in some representative industry. I daresay that a few weeks of this experience will give them more insight into some of the important problems of this generation than months spent in conning musty tomes. The professor who sits with them as counsellor when they meet in "classes" to share experiences, may challenge their conclusions, point out circumstances they have failed to observe, and suggest books and references by which they may supplement and broaden their experiences.

Necessarily, I believe, they will read far more prolifically and sincerely than they do now. To interpret their experiences as industrial workers they will have to consult not only the writings of the learned economists, but they must delve into history to find out how we get our present industrial order. Their quest for understanding might lead them to the fields of sociology, politics, even psychology, philosophy, geography, anthropology, histology, and ultimately to the "pure" sciences. And this is significant: they will see these fields not as pigeon-hole compartments of knowledge, but as a related unity affecting every act of our lives.

There may come the time when, as students broaden their experience by periodic occupations in the business world, the professor to keep apace with them, may find it necessary, in taking his Sabbatical leave of absence, to heed the example of Labor in demanding a five-day week, and demand for himself two free years in seven, one for research, and one for renewal of experience in the frantic world of commerce and industry. The professor of economics might well stitch seams in a garment factory; the criminologist, with no serious misuse of his time, might spend a few weeks in jail—possibly as an inmate; the dean of men, might divert his harassed mind from serious problems by directing traffic at some busy street intersection of some metropolis. This heretical suggestion may not prove necessary. Perhaps the professor may be able to maintain a sympathetic understanding of the forces that shape so much of our civilization today, while remaining aloof as a dispassionate observer. Nevertheless, I suggest it, half in jest, half in earnest, as a protest against the pedantry and closed-mindedness common among so many teachers today.

Working in industry, of course, is not the only way by which students may broaden their intellectual horizons. I stress it because I think through it, better than any other form of activity in the business world, students may become conscious of the ever-lasting problems of our society controlling the economic processes by which it lives.

Foreign travel should be strongly encouraged by the colleges. Unfortunately few students can afford it. Yet summer trips abroad may now be had almost as cheaply as a semester in college and, I believe, are wholly as valuable. Moreover, a dozen or so exchange scholarships might be created in every college; and closer relations between native and foreign students encouraged.

2. *Greater emphasis on personal development of students.* A college course should be appraised not by the number of facts dispensed by the professor and reported back to him in quizzes, but by what it does to the individual students enrolled. I believe that the lecture-quiz system must be supplanted by informal conferences between teachers and students, and group discussions, such as have proved so successful in many intercollegiate conferences. Those teachers will be most valuable who help the student to integrate his own experience, who can challenge him to new points of view, and guide him in his reading. Professors are not necessary chiefly as sources of information: students need to cultivate the habit of consulting source books for themselves.

Students, even as their elders, need to learn how to play: a disproportionate share of their recreation today is vicarious. The aims of creativity, and whole-hearted participation, can be served, I believe, through encouragement of intra-mural athletics. Commercialized athletics no doubt hinder this, but I see no immediate prospect of curtailing this Frankenstein. The experience of coöperative living in fraternities and sororities seems to me to counterbalance the unfortunate mental regimentation and snobbery that frequently results, but that is not inherent in the system.

3. *Democratic control of the college.* I justify this revolutionary proposal by John Dewey's phrase, "We learn by doing." I believe that students can become citizens of a democracy only through experience in democratic processes. I propose then a regency of tri-partite representation: students, faculty, and alumni, patrons, or the state.

These three steps in the reconstruction of the academic order, if and when achieved, I believe will go a long way toward the type of liberal education we have envisioned. But no one knows better than those immersed in the educational machinery, the slowness with which they will be made. The student in college today can find little consolation for present inadequacies in the thought of improved facilities a generation or so hence. He is face to face with the immediate problem of securing an education under prevailing circumstances.

He must begin by a reckless disregard of "courses," and a careful choice of professors. To a marked degree he may find it necessary to gain his education *sub rosa* by relying upon voluntary, and as yet unrecognized, means, such as the numerous intercollegiate conferences, summer industrial groups, and study tours to foreign countries. He may with advantage affiliate himself with intercollegiate organizations promoting vigorous thought on social questions, such as the youth section of the Fellowship of Reconciliation, the League for Industrial Democracy, or the Y. M. C. A. or Y. W. C. A. in those colleges where they have turned from an emphasis on theology to an emphasis on student problems. Student publications such as the New Student and the Intercollegian, and critical magazines like the Forum, the Nation, the New Republic, the World Tomorrow, Harper's, and the Survey, will broaden his national and world outlook.

This type of student will escape, I believe, the tragedy of the engineer, the technician, and the specialist whose knowledge is indispensable to the life of our highly industrialized society, yet who remain hirelings of shortsighted business men, and whose skill and ingenuity may be turned, at times, not to saving civilization, but to the wholesale destruction of it, as in war. But we are justified in believing that the student who has acquired a sense of social responsibility, who has learned to form his own judgments, and to evaluate a civilization by its fruits of human well-being, will avoid the niche of the intellectual Robot.

THE MEANING OF EDUCATION

Frank D. Slutz

'Am I getting an education? Such an inclusive and sweeping question needs to be broken up into subsidiary questions. What is an education? Can an education be "received," or must it be achieved? Must one either get an education or remain uneducated? Is this practice of "getting" an education now in vogue in our colleges? Why not? How many colleges inaugurate this practice? By answering these secondary questions, the primary question, "Am I getting an education?" will be simplified. It is to these subordinate questions that we now need to give attention.

What is an education? Most arguments, and most differences of opinion are, fundamentally, misunderstandings about the meaning of words and of terms. Education is one of those living, growing, changing words that well-nigh defy definition. At least an approximate definition may be attempted. An education is the ever-enlarging result of the continuous development of one's whole self (body, intelligence, personality, social responses, motives, ideals, tastes, skills) towards his maximum harmony with the truth of the universe and his usefulness in that universe. Does this definition sound bookish, pedantic? Is it practical and clear? Let the discussion below answer.

An education never ceases. The most dangerous word in our school parlance is "graduation." Education is hindered by graduation. Graduation is often a polite name for arrested development and stagnation. Education is, rightly, one commencement after another. The educated person should be like a tree planted by the rivers of water, bringing forth fruit increasingly in its season. The Master Teacher did not urge Nicodemus to be "born" again, but in the present sense of that verb he implied the need of being born again and again. Education is a procession of new births. Too few college graduates are readers. The practice of study is superseded by the pressing demands of business. Ask a hundred such college-trained men what they read and you will find that a popular magazine or two, a trade journal, the daily newspaper and occasionally a much advertized book make up their reading menu. Beyond the specialized education afforded by their vocation, by far the larger number of college graduates are not enjoying the thrilling experience of expanding intellectual horizons. For these men graduation was not a commencement but a completion of learning.

The current conception of education is that it concerns the academic, the intellectual areas of one's self. This idea dies hard! The soundest modern thinkers and leaders in education do not champion this old conception. They urge that education is not education unless it includes the whole self. A real and genuine education includes the body and its health; the training of the intelligence to master fundamental facts, to know where to find additional facts, to be skillful in interpreting facts, to be open always to new truth; education embraces the development of the personality, the control of the emotions, the selection of serviceable habits, the dismissal of habits that are nuisances, the cultivation of those individual capacities and powers which, contrary to the pronouncements of the behaviorists, do abide varyingly in different persons; an education worthy of the name must achieve self realization in that fine sense of realization which is true both to individual capacities and to the social good. Education has departed forever from the restricted area of "book learning"; not in that it discounts books, but in that it refuses to be limited by books.

Two items in this broad education of the whole self need to be stressed particularly: the education of the emotions and the principle that unlimited expression of instincts is not the road to happiness. The training of the intellect to the neglect of the emotions furnishes all too often for our times the spectacle of an efficient brain either made highly dangerous in the service of violent emotions, or frequently hindered and blunted by emotional maladjustment. Dr. Fosdick has asked more than once why, if the principle of free expression of instincts is sound, it is not applied to all the instincts alike; why, in a shipwreck a husky male is not applauded if he strikes down women and children, reaches a life boat, rides to safety and exults in the free expression of this instinct for self-preservation.

Education is not education at all if it leaves the one seeking it, or the one attaining a good measure of it, out of harmony with the truth of the universe. Education must bring with it truth in social relationships; tolerance of opinions; spiritual discovery; an escape from the arrogance that limits the universe to the hard and fast map of it that one may draw. One serious flaw in the old academic education was its failure to include within its scope those winnings of truth in such wholeness that the possessor was made free.

Education that does not make its achiever useful is surely a waste of time. Hamlet may have had that kind of an education. He could not act without infinite consideration, and long consideration made him powerless to act. When finally with headlong impetuosity he did act his performance was ill-timed, wasteful of life. Many fathers have, upon the graduation of their sons, sympathized understandingly with that pious parent who explained his share in the uselessness of his diploma-bearing boy by saying, like Aaron, "Behold I put in the gold and out came this calf." Education must increase one's desire and one's ability to serve; must connect him with that vocation which so fits his talents that it is at once his joy and his abounding opportunity.

A second question, under our main query is, Can an education be received or must it be achieved? Put in another form: Must one "get" his education?

The evidence is all in support of the statement that no one can accept an education. He can accept a degree! He can receive a diploma! An education must be won. Even information, which some confuse with education, cannot be received passively; some intensity of interest is necessary if information is to be retained. Education is what one has written into his practice, into his doing. A real musical education demands that its possessor shall play an instrument, or shall sing. Knowing about music, enjoying music which is heard—this is not education in music, this is information which enables one to appreciate music. Education for citizenship is nothing but a phrase unless one practices faithful, courageous, wise exercise of the franchise and unflinching bravery and high loyalty to ideals in office. Being informed about the machinery of government even to the minutest detail is only a fraction of the full distance to education for citizenship. No one is educated in French unless he can write and speak French properly and with ease. Our colleges should honor with degrees those who can produce poems. Instead, the degree of Doctor of Philosophy is given to those who, lacking in creative power, become skilled in criticizing and dissecting the poems of others. Small wonder that poets are rare among us! Huxley put this principle in unforgettable language when he said that an educated person is one who knows the laws of things and the laws of men and who obeys these laws with passionate devotion. Information is valuable but it is not enough; being informed is not being educated.

Now for a third question: If one must get his education, how may he get it?

Here is the deepest and the highest opportunity of the teacher! It is the prime skill of the teacher to induce students to want to learn, to love to learn, to long for knowledge. No boy or girl ever got much of an education by being compelled to study. Compulsion is able to drive the student to a knowledge of some of the rudiments of the tool subjects, reading, writing, and arithmetic. But an education begins with the birth of a hunger to learn. The teacher is one who fans this desire into a dominant passion. Once the student is on fire to know, then the teacher is ready to serve and to guide. What a great multitude of teachers are doomed to be Egyptian taskmasters, who grow gray and weary trying to force those without intellectual straw to make bricks of "credits"!

Teaching is scattering the contagion of knowing; teaching is guiding the pupil's mind into the high joys of learning. Teaching is companionship in learning. The major business of the teacher is to induce in his pupils the current of desire to know. This is the inescapable office and function of the teacher. Not a few boys are sent home from college because of those taskmaster teachers who cannot light any fire of enthusiasm in the hearts of the lads. No one ever will get an education, indeed no one is ever educated without the birth of a passion to learn. The world is full of informed persons; educated people are rarer.

Is the practice of "getting" an education now in vogue in our colleges? No. Not largely. Our shibboleths are standardization, tradition, information, routine, minutiæ, credits. When a student applies to a dean or a registrar for admission to college these days he is almost never asked "What do you think about this?" or "How would you meet this situation?" but "What credits have you to present?" Under our present academic practice, a class in swimming would be conducted in this manner: Around a fine and expensive swimming pool, benches would be erected. For five hours each week the students would assemble dressed in their bathing suits and surely bringing their notebooks. The teacher would lecture on the scissor's kick, the Australian crawl, the English side stroke and the breast stroke. Now and then he would have to chide his students for being inattentive and for looking longingly at the inviting water in the pool instead of at their notebooks. At the end of two semesters a rigid examination on the lectures would be given. Those making a grade of 60% would receive a diploma in swimming. Not a member of the class has been wet! In a shipwreck the only ones who would rescue themselves would be those who had secretly indulged out of hours and without permission in the sacred pool!

Dr. Coe, in "What Ails Our Youth," has said that much education is the throwing of pellets of information at youth arranged in classes; that the highest grades are given to those who can catch the largest number of these pellets and at examination time throw these pellets back to the teacher as demanded without having made any change in the pellets themselves. In "The Child, His Nature and His Needs," published by the Children's Foundation, Dr. M. V. O'Shea remarks that hitherto we have been conducting education to secure the maximum of likemindedness consistent with a minimum of the development of individual endowments; that we must do just the converse—we must educate for the maximum development of individual capacities consistent with the minimum of likemindedness.

Why is getting an education not a practice in American colleges? First, because of the vested interests of teachers in their favorite subjects. Long years of teaching any kind of subject matter develop a passion for that subject, and a stolid unwillingness to see it omitted from the educational menu. A second reason is that inertia operates with tremendous power in the educational institution. What has been done acquires the momentum of custom and the acceleration of tradition. Habit causes us to love convenience. Many a busy mother has said to her child, "Let me bake that pie! I can do it in half the time it takes to tell you how to do it!" This is the expression of the clutch of convenience. Our credit system, our examination system are splendidly efficient from the standpoint of administrative convenience. The pattern idea of quantity production has come over from the practice of manufacturing into the practice of education. Mass acceptance, mass treatment is made the order of procedure in dealing with persons. There is an insistence that personality is as completely amenable to quantity methods as things are. In business there must be advance adaptations, a vital prophylaxis that sees far ahead, that prepares for deep changes before they arrive. A business that fails to practice this foresight perishes. Education is often loath to make changes in its methods even after the crisis has arrived! We live in a world in which the status of women has changed rapidly in the last two decades; in which intimate personal ownership of business and tools has given place to long distance ownership; in which machines are no longer the hand-servants of men but almost the masters of men; in which leisure time is increasing apace; in which distance is all but cancelled; in which the nations no longer dwell as in a neighborhood but in one apartment house; in which a new authority, the authority of truth, is taking the place of the old authority of institutions; in which physical strain is excessive in the pressure of modern competition; in which there is arising a wide-spread feeling of superiority to law. In the face of all these characteristics of a modern day, a Freshman entering college in 1929 might take my old sheaf of sixteen credits that served as my educational passport in 1900 and every college door would open to him. One is tempted to ask if this condition indicates stability or only stagnation. We are yet laboring painfully under the illusion that school is not a place to learn but a place to be taught. For all these reasons, "getting" an education is not the accepted way of doing in the modern college.

So far the writer has probably been indulging in negative criticism. This has been necessary as a preface to the constructive suggestions that are now in order. How may the college inaugurate an enthusiastic getting of education in place of the present education by prescription?

The very first thing to be done is to call students into partnership in building educational plans. Students should have a wide share in the discussion of curricula, courses, policies, methods. Such partnership dissolves the hardened habit of prescription and opens education up to adventure, to exploration, to companionship in learning. A teacher is a little farther along in knowledge of the road to wisdom; he is not one who has arrived at complete wisdom. It is possible that the ease with which students cheat in examinations and in the preparation of notes might be made to disappear by the adoption of a policy of coöperative exploratory adventure as a substitute for the assignment method.

Is it not unwise to organize a college into departments? How often are the first two syllables of that word department accepted so loudly that isolation results! Depart! History departs from literature and literature departs from engineering! Each department is a little nation by itself, half rebellious towards the whole college. Students mark off department against department as if life were "faculty" phychology come to the fore again.

Would it not be better to build a college on a plan of "approachments" or of "entanglements," in place of departments? In the Survey for April 15, 1926, Dr. John H. Coffin, in an article headed "Making the Curriculum Fit the Man," has proposed an outline of such a plan. The various organized subjects could well be coördinated in a college offering the following approachments:

> Health;
> Citizenship;
> Leisure;
> Vocational Adjustment;
> Home Establishing;
> Life Philosophy.

History, literature, languages, sciences, mathematics are not ends in themselves; they are tools under the "approachments."

It is not enough to name these "approachments" and then to leave them. To do that would encourage their being made into "departments" as insulated from each other as those we now suffer. The scope and relationships of these "approachments" deserve further discussion, scant though it must be in the space here available. The most concise and suggestive method of the further analysis of these "approachments" will be that of asking questions which their study proposes:

1. Health:

> Is disease a physical misdemeanor?
>
> What comparative importance, in the achievement and maintenance of health do mental and physical hygiene have?
>
> How may the physical hardiness of cruder epochs be preserved in times of more complex civilization?
>
> What hidden practices in our civilization invite disease and degeneracy?
>
> What is the interplay of health and sex?
>
> What practices in the way of diet, exercise and sleep mean health for me, for my particular physical and mental organization?
>
> What subject matter, what science, has contributions to the study of health?
>
> What are the long-time effects of war on national health?
>
> What interest should nations and races have in the health of other nations and races?
>
> What of the proper balance of play and athletics?
>
> How may life be extended?

2. Citizenship:

> What has constituted citizenship in the various civilizations that make up world history?
>
> What are the elements of good citizenship in our times, in our country?
>
> How may public office be made more attractive and more genuinely serviceable?
>
> What are the forces that tend to make citizenship deteriorate?
>
> What is the future of the city in its relation to national government?
>
> What are the chief dangers that government and citizenship must face in the next quarter century?
>
> What are the mistakes of our democracy?
>
> Has suffrage a scientific basis?
>
> Have I any skill or ability that I owe my community?

3. Leisure:

What may be a sound philosophy of leisure? What is general and what for me?

What of leisure in the days ahead? Will it increase or decrease?

What are the dangers and the advantages of commercial appeals to the use of leisure time?

What are the social obligations of leisure?

What is the relation between one's vocation and his leisure?

What is leisure's obligation to culture?

What is the psychology of leisure?

4. Vocational Adjustment:

What criteria are available in determining vocational capacities?

What are the pressing vocational needs of the country?

Is it true that each person possesses one outstanding vocational ability?

Is it, instead, true that each person might do well in any one of a dozen generally related vocations?

Is one free to choose his vocation solely on the basis of his own desires and powers?

What is the scientific procedure for choosing a vocation?

What is my vocation to be?

What can one's vocation mean to his culture?

What vocations lie in the offing?

5. Home Establishing:

Is a home the primary achievement of one's life?

What do we know definitely of the laws of successful mating?

What was wrong with the old-fashioned home?

What shall the new home be like?

What of the employment of both husband and wife outside the home?

What of birth control?

How may the builders of splendid homes add their principles to our common knowledge?

Is marriage the climax of love or its beginning?

What is the relation among sex, love and character?

Is divorce or ignorant marriage our problem?

What is the truth about sex in and after marriage?

How may mates develop each other's personalities?

6. Life Philosophy:

What is the place of science and what, of a philosophy of life?

Are there any laboratory values in human experience?

What contributions have religions made to the meaning
of life? How valid are these contributions?

What is the case for materialism? For dualism? For
personalism? For idealism?

What problems in the meaning of life does psychology
present?

What shall we say of the self, of mind and brain?

Can life philosophies be judged by pragmatic tests?

Has science any function beyond the extension of the five
senses?

Is it not incomplete to know what the world is made of unless
we do our best to find out what it is made for? Again let it be
said that all subject matter is the servant, in interrelated fashion,
of these approachments. These subjects are like threads that
appear again and again in the fabric of the whole scheme; but no
subject is a woven pattern for its own sake. Such a pattern is
artificial.

Always there is the burden of the degree! Is a degree really
permissible if it signifies completion? Would it not be for the
advance of education at its best if a degree were like a dollar bill
torn in two, half being given to the Pullman porter at the beginning of a journey, and the other half at the end, provided the
service had been excellent? Could a provisional degree be granted
at the end of a college course, final confirmation of the degree
being reserved until the college had observed the provisionally
graduated student in action for a score of years? Is it not true
that A. B. may mean only what it does in a box score, "at bat"?
How can the runs, hits and errors be computed when the player
is just "at bat"?

Our college work is too often monastic, aloof, removed.
Katherine Lee Bates once said that every college provides two
streams of activity: the faculty stream of prescription, the student
stream of participation. Is it not true that the students sense
the lifelessness of much that holds in the academic areas of the
college and that they build up in defense a student life that
throbs with reality? Are not students eager to play any game
that is actual?

Educational improvements during the last twenty-five years
have had to do with the case, the dial, the hands, the crystal,
the finish of the educational watch; the same old escapement,
the same old movement within the watch operates unchanged.
The improvements have not been deep enough.

All educational paraphernalia is but a kit of tools. Buildings,
endowments, credits, curricula, programs, policies—all these are
tools. As long as the stars were made to serve the tools used in

their observation, astrology prevailed; when the stars were taken into partnership and when the tools served the stars, astronomy was born. Education will never be a science until all the tools are made subservient to what boys and girls, young men and young women, really are. Teachers grow petulant trying to make copper into concrete, maple into oak, and sponges into marble.

Right at this point we come face to face with one of the most serious charges against the colleges as they are. This charge is that college teachers as a whole (for there are magnificent exceptions) know their subjects far better than they know their pupils. They are like physicians skilled in the "materia medica" but knowing so little of anatomy that they cannot diagnose the faulty functioning of the organs. Scholarship is admirable, but a teacher must first of all be an expert in human engineering. If he is not his scholarship cannot function in his pupil's life. We may behold, if we will, a sad cumulative loss in our educational system. In the kindergartens and in the first and second grades of our elementary schools we have teachers who are past-masters in child psychology, making the whole school organization function for the pupils. Gradually, as we proceed in our investigation up through the grades, subject matter for its own sake usurps the throne of the child, until by the time we have advanced through the high school and into the college we find scholarship as the quite complete despot in the qualifications for teachers. Superintendent F. D. Boynton of the schools of Ithaca, New York, has thrown this deficiency as a challenge into the councils of our colleges.

A new day will have arrived when learners, acting in partnership with teachers, make education an adventure and a discovery.

Finally, no one can get an education by receiving information, by following a program of hours and units and courses. Am I getting an education? Am I a learner in my own right? Do I hunger and thirst after knowledge? Or do I hunger and thirst for credits, and for that glad day when, having accumulated the required number of points, and having run the examination gauntlet set by those who have survived similar gauntlets, I shall be officially excused from hungering and thirsting longer? The glorious truth is that no one ever gets an education, for once his hunger is whetted, he is never satisfied. For him, immortality will be but an extension of experience for indulging his divine discontent with what he knows. There is no such word as "Finis" in the lexicon of him who is getting an education.

SOVIET EDUCATION [1]

JOHN DEWEY

The idea of a school system in which pupils, and therefore studies and methods, are connected with social life instead of being isolated, is one familiar in educational theory. In some form, it is the idea that underlies all attempts at thorough-going educational reform. What is characteristic of Soviet education is not, therefore, the idea of a dovetailing of school activities into out-of-school social activities, but the fact that for the first time in history there is an educational system officially organized on the basis of this principle. Instead of being exemplified, as it is with ourselves, in a few scattering schools that are private enterprises, it has the weight and authority of the whole régime behind it. In trying to satisfy my mind as to how and why it was that the educational leaders have been able in so short a time to develop a working model of this sort of education, with so little precedent upon which to fall back, I was forced to the conclusion that the secret lay in the fact that they could give to the economic and industrial phase of social life the central place it actually occupies in present-day life. In that fact lies the great advantage the Revolution has conferred upon educational reformers in Russia in comparison with those in the rest of the world. I do not see how any honest educational reformer in western countries can deny that the greatest practical obstacle, in the way of introducing into schools the connection with social life that he regards as desirable, is the great part played by personal competition and desire for private profit in our economic life. This fact almost makes it necessary that in important respects school activities should be protected from social contacts and connections instead of being organized on the principle of instituting them. The Russian educational situation is enough to convert one to the idea that only in a society based upon the coöperative principle can the ideals of educational reformers be adequately carried into operation.

The central place of economic connections in the dovetailing of school work with social life outside the school is explicitly

[1] Published as an article in the *New Republic*, November, 1928, and reprinted with the kind permission of the editors and the author.

stated in the official documents of Commissar Lunarcharsky. He writes: "The two chief present problems of social education are: (1) The development of public economy with reference to social-ist reconstruction in general and the efficiency of labor in par-ticular; (2) The development of the population in the spirit of communism." The aims of education are set forth as follows: "(1) The union of general culture with efficiency of labor and power to share in public life; (2) Supply of the actual needs of national economy by preparation of workers in different branches and categories of qualifications; (3) Meeting the needs of dif-ferent localities and different kinds of workers."

Like all formal statements, these propositions have to be under-stood in the light of the practices by which they are carried into effect. So interpreted, the fact that among the aims the "union of general culture with efficiency of labor" precedes that of supply of special needs by preparation of workers assumes a significance that might not otherwise be apparent. For perhaps the striking thing in the system is that it is not vocational or industrial in the narrow sense those words often have with us, namely, the technical training of specialized workers. On the contrary, such training is everywhere postponed and subordinated to the require-ments of general culture which is, however, itself conceived of in a socially industrial sense; that is to say, as discovery and develop-ment of the capacities that enable an individual to carry on in a coöperative way work that is socially useful, "socially useful" being conceived in the generous sense of whatever makes human life fuller and richer. Perhaps the easiest way to grasp the spirit of the industrial connections of school work with general social activities is to take the utterances of our own Manufacturers' Association on the same topic and then reverse them. Preparation for special occupations is deferred to the stage of special schools called *Technicums,* which can be entered only after seven years of the public "unified" school have been completed. These schools are called "polytechnic" in character, but the word is a misleading one in its ordinary English associations. For with us it signifies a school in which individual pupils can select and pursue any one of a considerable number of technologies, while in the Russian system it signifies a school in which pupils, instead of receiving a "mono-technical" training, are instructed in the matters which are fundamental to a number of special industrial techniques. In other words, even in the definitely vocational schools, specialized training for a particular calling is postponed until the latest years, after a general technological and scientific-social foundation has been laid.

As far as could be determined, there are two causes for the adoption of this broad conception of industrial education in its identification with general culture appropriate to a coöperatively conducted society. One is the state of progressive educational theory in other countries, especially in the United States, during the early formative years after the Revolution. For a leading principle of this advanced doctrine was that participation in productive work is the chief stimulus and guide to self-educative activity on the part of pupils, since such productive work is both in accord with the natural or psychological process of learning and provides the most direct road to connecting the school with social life, because of the part played by occupations in the latter. Some of the liberal Russian educators were carrying on private experimental schools on this basis before the Revolution; the doctrine had the prestige of being the most advanced among educational philosophies and it answered to immediate Russian necessities.

Thus from an early period the idea of the "school of work" (*Arbeitschule, école du travail, escuela d'acción*) was quite central in post-revolutionary school undertakings. And a main feature of this doctrine was that, while productive work is the educative factor par excellence, it must be taken in a broad social sense, and as a means of creating a social new order and not simply as an accommodation to the existing economic régime.

This factor, however, accounts only for the earlier period of the growth of Soviet education, say up to 1922 or 1923, a period when American influence along with that of Tolstoi was upon the whole predominant. Then there came in a reaction from a Marxian standpoint. The reaction, however, did not take the form of discarding the notion of productive work as central in schools. It only gave the idea a definitely socialistic form by interpreting the idea of work by means of the new estate of the worker brought about by the proletarian revolution. The change was a more or less gradual one, and even now there is hardly a complete transition or fusion. But the spirit of the change is well indicated in the words of one of the leaders of educational thought: "A school is a true school of work in the degree in which it prepares the students to appreciate and share in the ideology of the workers—whether country or city." And by the worker is here meant, of course, the worker made conscious of his position and function by means of the revolution. This transformation of the earlier "bourgeois reforming idea," through its emphasis upon the ideology of the labor movement, thus continued and reinforced the earlier emphasis upon the general as part of the connection of the school with industry at the expense of merely specialized technical training.

This report is necessarily confined to a statement of general principles: the skeleton would gain flesh and blood if space permitted an account of the multifarious threads by which the connection between the schools and cooperatively organized society is maintained. In lieu of this account I can only pay my tribute to the liberating effect of active participation in social life upon the attitude of students. Those whom I met had a vitality and a kind of confidence in life—not to be confused with mere self-confidence—that afforded one of the most stimulating experiences of my life. Their spirit was well reflected in the inscription which a boy of fourteen wrote upon the back of a painting he presented me with. He was in one of the schools in which the idea just set forth is most completely and intelligently carried out, and he wrote that the picture was given in memory of the "school that opened my eyes." All that I had ever, on theoretical grounds, believed as to the extent to which the dull and dispirited attitude of the average school is due to isolation of school from life was more than confirmed by what I saw of the opposite in Russian schools.

There are three or four special points that call for notice in the identification established between cultural and industrialized education. One of them is suggested by the official statement regarding meeting by the schools of local conditions and needs. Soviet education has not made the mistake of confusing unity of education with uniformity: on the contrary, centralization is limited to the matter of ultimate aim and spirit, while in detail diversification is permitted, or rather encouraged. Each province has its own experimental school, that supplements the work of the central or federal experimental stations, by studying local resources, materials, and problems with a view to adapting school work to them. The primary principle of method officially laid down is that in every topic work by pupils is to begin with observation of their own environment, natural and social. The best museum of natural and social materials for pedagogical purposes I have ever seen is in the country district outside of Leningrad, constructed on the basis of a complete exhibit of local fauna, flora, mineralogy, etc., and local antiquities and history, made by pupils' excursions under the direction of their teachers. This principle of making connections with social life on the basis of starting from the immediate environment is exemplified on its broadest scale in the educational work done with the minority populations of Russia—of which there are some fifty different nationalities. The idea of cultural autonomy that underlies political federation is made a reality in the schools. Before the Revolution, many, most of them had no schools, and a considerable number of them not even a written language. In about ten years, through enlisting the efforts of anthropologists and linguistic scholars—in which branch of science Russia has always been strong—all the different languages have been reduced to written form, text-books in the local language provided, each adapted to local environment and industrial habits, and at least the beginnings of a school system introduced. Aside from immediate educational results, one is impressed with the idea that the scrupulous regard for cultural independence characteristic of the Soviet régime is one of the chief causes of its stability, in view of the non-communist beliefs of most of these populations. Going a little further, one may say that the freedom from race and color prejudice characteristic of the régime is one of the greatest assets in Bolshevist propaganda among Asiatic peoples. The most effective way to counteract the influence of that propaganda would be for western nations to abandon their superiority-complex in dealing with Asiatic populations, and thereby deprive Bolshevism of its contention that capitalism, imperialistic exploitation and race prejudice are so inseparably conjoined that the sole relief of native peoples from their lies is adoption of communism under Russian auspices.

The central place of human labor in the education scheme is made manifest in the plan for the selection and organization of subject matter, or the studies of the curriculum. This principle is officially designated the "complex system." In general the system means, on the negative side, the abandonment of splitting up subject matter into isolated "studies," such as form the program in the conventional school, and finding the matter of study in some total phase of human life—including nature in the relations it sustains to the life of man in society. Employing the words of the official statement: "At the basis of the whole program is found the study of human work and its organization: the point of departure is the study of this work as found in its local manifestations." Observations of the latter are, however, to be developed by "recourse to the experience of humanity—that is, books, so that the local phenomena may be connected with national and international industrial life." It is worthy of note that in order to carry out this conception of the proper subject matter of study, it is necessary for the teachers themselves to become students, for they must conceive of the traditional subject matter from a new point of view. They are compelled, in order to be successful, to study both their local environment and to become familiar with the detailed economic plans of the central government. For example, the greatest importance is attached in the educational scheme to natural science and what we call nature-study. But according to the ruling principle, this material must be treated not as so much isolated stuff to be learned by itself, but taken up in the ways in which it actually enters into human life by means of the utilization of natural resources and energies in industry for social purposes. Aside from the vitalization of physical knowledge supplied by thus putting it in its human context, this method of presentation compels teachers to be cognizant of the *Gosplan*—that is, the detailed projects, looking ahead over a series of years, of the Government for the economic development of the country. An educator from a bourgeois country may well envy the added dignity that comes to the function of the teacher when he is taken into partnership in the plans for the social development of his country. Such an one can hardly avoid asking himself how far this partnership is possible of existence only in a country where industry is a public function rather than a private undertaking; he may not find any sure answer to the question but the continued presence of the query in his mind will surely serve as an eye-opening stimulus.

In American literature regarding Soviet education, the "complex system" is often identified with the "project method" as that has developed in our own country. In as far as both procedures get away from starting with fixed lessons in isolated studies, and substitute for it endeavor to bring students through their own activity into contact with some relatively total slice of life or nature, there is ground for the identification. By and large, however, it is misleading and for two reasons. In the first place, the complex method involves a unified intellectual scheme of organization: it centers, as already noted, about the study of human work in its connection on one side with natural materials and energies, and on the other hand with social and political history and institutions. From this intellectual background, it results that while Russian educators acknowledge here—as in many other things—an original indebtedness to American theory, they criticize many of the "projects" employed in our schools as casual and as trivial, because they do not belong to any general social aim or have definite social consequences in their train. To them, then, an educative "project" is the means by which the principle of some "complex" or unified whole of social subject matter is realized. Its criterion of value is its contribution to some "socially useful work." Actual projects vary according to special conditions, urban or rural, and particular needs and deficiencies of the local environment. In general, they include contributions to improvement of sanitation and hygienic conditions, in which respects there is an active campaign carried on modelled largely upon American techniques, assisting in the campaign against illiteracy; reading newspapers and books to the illiterate; helping in clubs, excursions, etc., with younger children, assistance of ignorant adults to understand the policies of local soviets so that they can take part in them intelligently; engaging in communist propaganda, and, on the industrial side, taking some part in a multitude of

diverse activities calculated to improve economic conditions. In a rural school that was visited, for example, students carried on what in a conventional school would be the separate studies of botany and entomology by cultivating flowers, food-plants, fruits, etc., under experimental conditions, observing the relation to them of insects, noxious and helpful, and then making known the results to their parents and other farmers, distributing improved strains of seed, etc. In each case, the aim is that sooner or later the work shall terminate in some actual participation in the larger social life, if only for younger children carrying flowers to an invalid or to their parents. In one of the city schools where this work has been longest carried on, I saw, for example, interesting charts that showed the transformation of detailed hygienic and living conditions of the homes in a workingmen's quarter effected through a period of ten years by the boys and girls of the school.

A word regarding the system of administration and discipline of Soviet schools perhaps finds its natural place in this connection. During a certain period, the idea of freedom and student control tended to run riot. But apparently the idea of "auto-organization," which is fundamental in the official scheme, has now been worked out in a positive form, so that upon the whole the excesses of the earlier period are obsolescent. The connection with what has just been said lies in the fact that as far as possible the organization of pupils that are relied upon to achieve self-discipline are not created for the sake of school "government," but grow out of the carrying on of some line of work needed in the school itself or in the neighborhood. Here, too, while the idea of self-government developed in American schools was an originally stimulating factor, the ordinary American practice is criticized as involving too much imitation of adult political forms, instead of growing out of the students' own social relationships, and hence as being artificial and external. In view of the prevailing idea of other countries as to the total lack of freedom and total disregard of democratic methods in Bolshevist Russia, it is disconcerting, to say the least, to anyone who has shared in that belief, to find Russian school children much more democratically organized than are our own; and to note that they are receiving through the system of school administration a training that fits them much more systematically than is attempted in our professedly democratic country for later active participation in the self-direction of both local communities and industries.

Fairness demands that I should say in conclusion that the educational system so inadequately described exists at present qualitatively rather than quantitatively. Statistically considered, its realization is still highly restricted—although not surprisingly so when one considers both the external difficulties of war, famine, poverty, teachers trained in alien ideas and ideals, and the internal difficulties of initiating and developing an educational system on a new social basis. Indeed, considering these difficulties, one is rather amazed at the progress already made; for while limited in actual range, the scheme is in no sense on paper. It is a going concern; a self-moving organism. While an American visitor may feel a certain patriotic pride in noting in how many respects an initial impulse came from some progressive school in our own country, he is at once humiliated and stimulated to new endeavor to see how much more organically that idea is incorporated in the Soviet system than in our own. Even if he does not agree with the assertion of communist educators that the progressive ideals of liberal educators can actually be carried out only in a country that is undergoing an economic revolution in the socialist direction, he will be forced into searchings of heart and mind that are needed and wholesome. In any case, if his experience is at all like mine, he will deeply regret those artificial barriers and that barricade of false reports that now isolate American teachers from that educational system in which our professed progressive democratic ideas are most completely embodied, and from which accordingly we might, if we would, learn much, more, much more than from the system of any other country. I understand now as I never did before the criticisms of some foreign visitors, especially from France, that condemn Soviet Russia for entering too ardently upon an "Americanization" of traditional European culture.

A CONSTRUCTIVE CRITICISM OF MODERN EDUCATION

J. STITT WILSON

The universe has been carrying on for a long time a great school for living creatures, and it is compulsory education with a vengeance. Amœba and caterpillar, fish and bird, dog, ape and man—all must go to the same stern schoolmaster. Life is no respecter of persons.

And in some respects the task was being well done before we built the little red school house and started in to help. The bee has turned out to be quite an expert architect. The albatross had Lindbergh beaten ages ago. The salmon knows how to leap the cataract and find the spawning places. The fleet-footed creatures, the keen-scented, the long-headed provident ones—all seem to have gone to good schools and to have received their diplomas— they make good. Natural selection and the laws of survival seem to preclude any "easy credits" or "snap courses." There is no getting-by. The law seems to be, pass nature's examination or perish.

And for man no exception was made. He is no darling of nature, if the anthropologists speak truly. Indeed it would almost seem as if the schoolmaster had treated him more roughly than any other creature. Early man had a thin skin, he was slow of foot, with only moderate powers of scent and many other handicaps. Nature seemed to say: "Here Son! I have stood you up on your hind legs. I have given you a little extra gray matter, and I have given you a sense of humor, so you can laugh at yourself. Get into my school with its labor and reward and punishment and make good or perish."

The whole world is thrown open for man. He is led into the picture galleries of the universe—sun, moon, stars; mountains and plains, rivers and oceans; sunrise and sunset; the marvellous seasons! He is escorted deep down into the secret places and left there in jeopardy to search his way out. He is tantalized by mystery and tragedy and left to guess through his blinding tears "the riddle of the universe." With climate, with beasts, with men more deadly than beasts, he fought his way. It was a great school and hard; a school of discipline most severe; but man learned. He passed many a hard examination after semesters ages long.

Came the hunt, and the herd, and the tilled soil, and the city. He roamed, he fought, he preyed, and he prayed. Medicine men and soothsayers, prophets and priests, sages and seers, herded him and instructed him. They quieted him with superstitions, or soothed his fears with half-truths.

Man's greatest educators are his institutions—the family, the tribe, the government, the religious cult and developing industry. These he made, and in turn these made him. Under a "cake of custom" repeatedly hardening over his evolving being, he wriggled and writhed and grew for centuries. These institutions were his great teachers, training and drilling him. By fear, by necessity, by lure, by slavery he was instructed.

Came Babylon, and Thebes and Greece and Rome. Came the great masters—Confucius, Buddha, Moses, Socrates, Jesus— crying in the wilderness of man's ignorance. Finally came Galileo, Newton, Faraday, Einstein—the sons of the age of science, teaching man to study his world and master it.

As for us moderns, we have created the greatest of all institutions, the public school, the high school, and the university, as a system of popular education. We have undertaken this task of the education of man, taking the child from the cradle, teaching him, training him, and placing him amid the manifold meanings of human existence in the various institutions of human society. Man is the creature unfinished, who seeks thus to remake himself. Manifestly, the proper education of such a complex being, in such a complex society, and for such a mysterious destiny is no simple matter. True education must be as complex as the nature of man and the nature of the universe. Education must be based on psychology, and psychology roots in biology and looks to all the meanings of life.

There are at least three principal phases or aspects of this complex process. Perhaps we might draw an equilateral triangle, and let each side represent one of these phases. Or we might describe a circle and let three approximately equal arcs represent these aspects of one complete process. A careful consideration of these three phases of education, should reveal the importance of each and our over-emphasis or our neglect. Such a study should appreciate that which we have done, and take note of that which we have left undone. Such a treatment should be a constructive criticism of modern education.

1. EDUCATION FOR EFFICIENCY

The first phase of human education is *Education for Efficiency.* The amazing amount of information that a little child can accumulate without learning to read and write is a hint to us in educational method. However, we proceed with our three R's. They are the simplest tools of our culture and remain so to the end. These three R's are the beginnings of education in efficiency. By them we learn what has been achieved in the past, we are able to communicate to others, and we lay the foundation of all science—that is, we measure. Then this process is extended. We learn the languages. We try to know the story of our race. We begin to learn the lessons of nature and the creations of art that have enriched mankind.

As the centuries have passed, and civilization has become more complex and highly specialized, education for efficiency has become more and more important. Probably in the minds of most students in school and college today, the main idea is to prepare for life, for a job, for a position.

About three centuries ago there occurred the great revolution in the education of man—a revolution which placed education for efficiency on the throne of the whole process. For over a thousand years education in the western world had been dominated by the principle of authority. Certain ideas, opinions, doctrines, dogmas, were determined. Argument might follow only inside these prescribed limits and accepted principles. For the most part men ran round and round in their little circles of accepted ideas for a long millenium, until the human spirit was virtually imprisoned in ignorance and superstition. Neither freedom nor progress was possible. Education tended to stultification.

Then came a small group of great thinkers. "Beware," says Emerson, "when the Lord lets loose a great thinker in the earth." These men took up an eraser as it were, and ruthlessly rubbed out well-nigh the whole educational system of the past. The more men examined the old system the more they were filled with disgust. Among the first of these educational revolutionists was Francis Bacon, who was followed by Descartes. Of the Aristotelian Greeks Bacon complained: "They assuredly have that which is characteristic of boys; they are prompt to prattle but cannot generate; for their wisdom abounds in words but is barren of works. From all these systems of the Greeks, and their ramifications through particular sciences, there can hardly after the lapse of so many years be adduced a single experiment which tends to relieve and benefit the condition of man."

That last phrase is the key to the whole revolution. The Baconian spirit, as manifested in all these reformers, demanded useful knowledge, to benefit the condition of man. According to Bacon true education consisted in observing the facts of nature, discovering its laws, and then harnessing these laws to do our will. Thus we would no longer be victims but masters. We should have power over all the forces of nature. Thus we may enter into the true kingdom of man. This alone is real education, said the Baconians—education for utility, for efficiency, for power.

Compared with all previous history this modern period of science since Bacon seems a miracle of human achievement. Came Copernicus, Galileo, Kepler, Newton, Faraday, Darwin, Einstein. Came the great inventors with their mighty machines, giant ocean liners, transcontinental railroads, the printing press, electricity harnessed in a hundred ways—the aeroplane, the radio, television, synthetic chemistry! It would at first appear that Bacon and Descartes had discovered the final secret and key to the education of man. One hesitates to question these herculean tasks of modern science. The whole universe seems aching for disclosure to the mind of man as scientist. And doubtless all our modern scientific and mechanical achievements are but the little ante-room of that sublime palace which yet awaits man. The press reports that President Max Mason, who has resigned the presidency of the University of Chicago to become research director of the Rockefeller Foundation, visions a world free of hunger, poverty, and sickness, and even of morbid worries and unsound passions, whenever knowledge becomes sufficient and is made available to the people.

Yet as we have already said man is a highly complex being and his education should be as complex as his nature. And education for efficiency alone will not suffice. To make this the goal and objective of our whole education is to lose our way and come to tragedy. It is not enough to know the laws of nature, and harness nature's powers to our will. We might arrive, indeed have we not arrived already at the place where as Emerson said, "things are in the saddle and ride mankind"? Like Frankenstein we have called monsters into being and they have enslaved us. Despite all our mighty mechanical devices and our consequent material prosperity, the masses of men are still poor and sometimes slaves. The Middle Ages of the old education were dark indeed, but what could be more sordid than Pittsburgh, and West Virginia, or the slums of New York and Liverpool, Paris and Berlin? What crushing human problems confront the industrial workers who make and tend all these mighty machines.

And War! What war of man against man could conceivably be so unutterable as that for which we are now preparing with our perfected science—bombs slaying non-combatants with their deadly gases; aeroplanes like devastating demons of destruction annihilating whole sections of a population.

Have we not abused our triumph over Nature? Has our education for efficiency been perverted until we are turning ourselves into standardized mechanical "Robots," thus to create a purely materialistic civilization where our only gods are money and power and material success? Are we like children playing with edged tools to our moral as well as our physical danger? Consider how threatening are the social and economic problems of the world today. Even the boasted prosperity of the United States is accompanied by social injustices of a very serious character. We have not reached the stage where these evils have become as acute as in some other lands. But the end is not yet. So grave is the struggle of the producing classes in many countries of the world that social revolution is not impossible, despite, or rather because of, the mechanical conquest of nature, through education for power, which has lost its way and has made us idolaters of the work of our own hands.

Is it too much to say that much of our higher education today is a round of learning by rote, of parrot work for bromide minds, producing cogs for this machine age? Something is lacking. Many seniors at college are aware of it. Many feel they have a smattering of many things and not much of anything. Their education is in spots. It is not creative. Education for efficiency pushed to the extreme, as if it were the whole of the education of man, produces starved and anemic personalities, lacking in educational vitamines.

Bacon himself feared some such result. It is a mark of his far-reaching insight, when, in the preface of his "Novum Organum," he prayed that "from the opening of the pathway of the senses and a fuller kindling of the natural light, there may not result in man's soul a weakening of faith and a blindness to the divine mysteries." Commenting on this, Irving Babbitt suggests that Bacon himself became the victim of this educational error: "The significance of Bacon's moral breakdown lies in the very fact that it had the same origins as his idea of progress. Bacon was led to neglect the human law through a too subservient pursuit of the natural law; in seeking to gain dominion over things he lost dominion over himself. He is a notable example of how a man may be 'un-kinged' as Emerson phrases it, when over-mastered by the naturalistic temper and unduly fascinated by power and success. Bacon was aware that material progress so far from assuring moral progress, may actually imperil man's higher nature."

L. P. Jacks in his recent book on "Constructive Citizenship" voices a warning against this over-emphasis in scientific education for power and efficiency. He says: "If science be nothing more than a short-cut to our ends, a labor-saving device, a means of satisfying the desire for 'happiness' with the minimum of effort and personal skill till man's vocation as a worker becomes a mere affair of pressing buttons and turning switches—if that be all, then I for one will say: 'Let the hour stand accursed when science was born into the world'!" He says that the most popular conception of science today is that it is the mighty instrument which enables man to conquer nature and develop her resources for his own advantage—to distil the universe into our happiness. Such conceptions, he considers, are "shallow, and profoundly irreligious, whose ultimate effect if we persist in them can be nothing else than to turn us into a race of scientific blackguards, on whom, we may be sure outraged nature will know how to revenge herself—as, indeed, if we consider the matter attentively, she has long been doing." That is certainly a serious impeachment of a false emphasis or perversion of the place of science in the education of man.

If, therefore, education is for the real efficiency of the whole man it must press on and include the deeper aspects of his nature, his relation to society, and his spiritual vocation and destiny. Information is not education, and mere power over nature for our material advantage will not suffice.

2. CREATIVE EDUCATION

Several years ago I took the courses of study offered in this country by Dr. Maria Montessori, the noted Italian educator. Although I had always been deeply interested in those educational processes that tended to free the native powers and gifts of the individual, the Montessori method came to me as a much needed emphasis. By contrast, much of our educational procedure seemed like a mechanical process, designed to make little human cogs for a machine civilization. It is as if we were feeding our children into a great educational mill out of which they come standardized to a pattern, drilled to a type, for the imitative processes of our industrial and social life.

The organization of modern industry, with its extreme division of labor and mass production has doubtless affected our entire educational system. This is particularly so since the inauguration of compulsory education. The armies of students entering high school and college compel mass methods. We now have single university classes enrolling a thousand students. And when it is remembered that "business" stands at the door of the school from the grades to the university to take the youth, expecting him to be already an apprentice, and ready to put him into his place in the great mechanism of industry and finance, what can we expect but standardized educational products?

The whole educational process should be as a mother brooding over her children, bringing out of each child his or her particular aptitude and releasing native and original talent. The real teacher is not simply one who can skillfully impart information, but is one who discovers the original and creative powers of the student, and knows how to cooperate with the growing mind to bring it to expression.

If human life were only the making of a living, education for efficiency would suffice. But life is more than that. Life is expression. At best life is art. And art is joy. In fact there is no joy without art, without self-expression. Every teacher who observes childlife knows that pupils are altogether the happiest, not when they are merely getting lessons and preparing to recite or cramming for examinations, in the hunt for credits, but when they have conceived some original idea, of hand, or head, or heart, and have put forth their own native powers to bring it into being.

It would seem absurd to harp on this string if it were not for the tragedy of herd-schooling, tread-mill work, imitative procedure, credit-chasing, degree-getting, and standardized experience that is so prevalent at the present time.

All the really great educators took high ground concerning creative education. Froebel felt that we were not educating the child unless we were seeking its "perfect evolution in accord with the laws of its being." He wanted "self-completion" in the child rather than "getting on in the world." He recognized that one could be educated for efficiency and be a "success," while the native powers of the soul were being atrophied. This was also the claim of Dr. Montessori. It is the heart of the project method. It is the root meaning of the very word, education.

I might have called this phase, education for freedom, education for self-discovery, education for originality. But I have used the words "Creative Education" partly because of the recent notable contribution on this subject by Henry Fairfield Osborn. Dr. Osborn came to the conclusion that something has been lost in the art of education, and that a great principle needs re-discovery. That principle if found would release original and creative intelligence. He says that "except in practical inventions for the welfare of man, our general creative powers are almost at a standstill; we depend more and more on inventions and creations of the gifted few." He fears the effects of our modern machine age with its stifling of observation and creative powers and warns us against it. He complains that "from the standpoint of the lofty creative aim of education the present prospects in America are far from bright, because the imitative element in our civilization is dominant." Our tendency is to produce the parrot-mind, the bromidic mind. "Original and creative power in the germ," says Osborn, "is the very oldest of the distinctively human faculties, and the cultivation and development of these powers should be the chief end of education to which all others should contribute."

This aspect of creative education is most perfectly represented in our great scientific discoverers and creative artists, poets, painters and sculptors. In great minds like Galileo, Newton, Leonardo da Vinci, Michaelangelo, Raphael, Shakespeare, Whitman, free creative genius comes to its most perfect expression. The emotions, the imagination, the very blood and nerve—the whole man—are free and released for original creation, free to depart from routine, to enter new fields, to create new standards, to leave the beaten paths, to escape the thrall of conventionalized existence, and give the whole mind and spirit expression.

Common mortals should receive a type of education that would be to us in our measure what the expression of their genius was to these great ones in their larger measure. Our minds and hearts, our emotions and feelings, our will and purpose should be set free to do original work, to express independent thought. This luxury of creation, this bliss of being, should not be the special privilege of genius while we trudge on in beaten paths, or in the deep ruts made for our feet by dead men and the rigorous institutions of history.

And what of all the little children, of adolescent youth, and our college men and women? Shall we put them into our educational harness? Shall we drill them with our efficiencies? Shall we buckle them into shapes ready for the masters of our industrial civilization, to be harnessed like docile beasts of burden to the machines that will still further stultify them? No! Education—all of it—from the mother's knee to the last attainment of post-graduate study should make free. It should brood over original powers and release them; it should woo the soul forth into its due manifestation. Where are the teachers who shall so educate the youth of the world?

In our educational system tradition orders. The individual obeys. The type is created, and thousands never know what manner of men they might have been. Emerson wrote of one who was "born a man and died a grocer." These youths are born human beings, and are trained into college students. All of this must be said, of course, with large exceptions. But Osborn's criticism stands. Imitation is dominant even to tyranny.

We have the revelation of the need of this creative education in the very spirit of youth which is often condemned. The craving for adventure, for daring faith that does not question what dangers may lie ahead, the disregard of inhibitions and repressions, the easy neglect of customs and conventions by youth—

what are these but phases of creative life, bent on expression, acknowledging the Lord of Life only, and rejecting all other gods, following the gleam of promise that somewhere there is fullness of life. Youth simply cannot stand the mediocre, the commonplace, the gray and the drab. If in some way we could let their nonchalance and independence find genuine creative expression, we would save them from many a folly and enrich the world by their contributions. Idleness, ennui, boredom, "getting by," and the rest will be reduced when creative education comes into its own with modern youth. No day is too long for the artist's passion or for creative labor.

A real education, moreover, should be the inspiration for revolt against the over-standardization which so often curses our modern life. Real education should mark a man by lifting him out of the herd. Originality of thought and action, freedom of expression, daring of spirit to live one's own life, intellectual and moral adventure—these should be the sure signs that a man or woman has been a candidate for higher education and has acquired it.

If creative education held sway on equal terms with education for efficiency, we would more often see the release of daring spirits, free souls, creators and deliverers among teachers and students. Our whole public life would then feel the purging power of a more emancipated public opinion.

3. THE CULTURE OF THE HUMAN SPIRIT IN THE EXPERIENCE OF GOD

I now come to the third phase of the education of man. After ten years of constant work in the colleges and a long association with students, I know their sensitiveness on matters of religion and their impatience with traditional sectarianism. For the moment, let us not ask what is the duty or responsibility of the school or the college for the religious education of our youth. Let us think, as we did in the first place, of man, and his culture and training, irrespective of how he gets it or who provides it. Let us forget for a moment every creed or doctrine that men have written or believed. Knowing what we now know, of man, of his history, of his institutions, of his long progressive evolution, can we consider a man "educated"—no matter what he knows, no matter how skilled in technique, or trained in science, no matter how gifted he may be—if he is dishonorable, or corrupt, or perverted in character? Grant that it is extremely difficult to work out a true philosophy of life, or a pure religion free from superstition, nevertheless, is it conceivable that we can consider the education adequate that does not definitely stimulate those lofty elements of spiritual character, which we instinctively honor and praise as we see them embodied in the great souls that have been the glory of the human race? Can we say that the educational process is doing a satisfactory work for youth when it merely trains the intellect, or develops skill? What about the characters in history that stood up for the poor and the oppressed, fought for justice against human tyrants, died fighting for truth against ignorance in church and state, establishing the Kingdom of God in some measure amidst the wrongs and tragedies of our race?

There were great minds in ancient Greece. Of these Socrates was near the summit in all the culture of Athens. But the outstanding quality of the education of that great sage of antiquity is revealed in his lofty character, in his penetrating spiritual vision, in his sublime moral courage. Socrates drinking the hemlock—that is the educated Socrates. It is said that he taught that all that men needed was "to know." But Socrates meant a knowing that should bear fruit in an education that disciplines and purifies character, that spiritualizes and energizes the whole personality.

It is almost impossible to speak of Jesus of Nazareth without the association of some traditional pattern that hides or distorts the real figure. "Is not this the carpenter's son?" "Whence hath he this wisdom?" Was Christ really educated? Do we see in his spirit, his attitudes, his words, his behavior, a phase of the education of the human spirit that ought to be the goal of man? Here was dignity without pride, heroism without boasting, power accompanied by tenderest kindness, marvelous historic insight, understanding clear as sunlight, intellectual genius, balance of judgment. Is this education? This man of Galilee devoted his life utterly to humanity. He stood up for truth against falsehood and hypocrisy. He incarnated justice and mercy in a cruel age. He collided with popular opinion, with organized priestcraft and greedy money-changers, and with a courage that only devotion to the highest can manifest, he faced arrest as a felon, went through a mockery of a trial, and came to a friendless end on a lonely cross. It takes blood, red blood, to live that sort of life. No bravado, no spasmodic goodness, no petty virtue is equal to that quality of sustained moral courage. Here is suggested a phase of the education of man that the world needs today as never before.

Laying aside for the moment all theological controversy, there is such a thing as goodness of character, spiritual understanding, and moral heroism amidst the evils and injustice of our evolving race. *And no education is true education that ignores or neglects or makes this subordinate in the life of youth.* If we sow to the wind we shall reap the whirlwind. I have called this third phase "the culture of the human spirit in the experience of God." I am trying to avoid soft or inadequate words. I believe that this language will stand the strain of the scientific revolution through which the world is still passing, and the religious revolution that is impending. By the experience of God is meant all the possibilities of ethical living, spiritual understanding and mystical illumination. True education should include such spiritual experience. The word *experience* is pertinent to a scientific age, it is immediate, personal and experimental. It suggests the pragmatic. It has to do with actual realities in living rather than with mere theories and ideas.

Eventually it may be found that the most immediate and most intimate experience of any human being is the experience of God. We think we have experience of ourselves in self-consciousness. Quite possibly what we call self-consciousness may be our egoistic way of describing the Life of the Infinite as revealed in us. We think we have experience of nature, of its principles and powers. May not this grand expanding science be but a glimpse of the garment of God? Is not the radio a hint of omnipresence and omniscience?

Here in Nature is apparently infinite power and infinite intelligence, and Life! Life!—bursting out of reservoirs unutterable! Here is Good ineffable, sustaining, nourishing.

Is it thinkable that we human beings have independently any life in ourselves, any intelligence, any power? "In that Power, Life, and Intelligence—infinitely and immediately enveloping us—we live and move and have our being." Our immediate senses of sight and hearing are impossible except as linked and cooperative with that Power and Presence. Can it be otherwise than that the meaning of our lives—the education of man—is in our appropriation of that Life and Power, our entering more and more into cooperative existence in the one Life and the one Intelligence?

As the unborn child appropriates life from its mother so are we all nourished and sustained in God. As the child later seeks its mother's breast, so do we cry like an infant in the night for the living God. And as the growing child and youth, with advancing intelligence cooperates with parents, with nature, and society, and by his adjusted behavior, enters into more and more abundant living, so, man's supreme education, voluntarily undertaken, and successfully achieved is the intelligent cooperation of his behavior with the Divine—the experience of God.

Temporarily the youth of our times are in no slight degree robbed of this supreme education. Many parents of today have not themselves sufficient experience to share it intelligently with their children. We have so separated church and state that we do not boldly and efficiently make the school or the university a spiritual educator of our youth. We are all awaiting a new breath from heaven. Meantime youth lives on, often accepting easy or demoralizing philosophies, or they drift, awaiting some later vision. The churches also are in transition and often do not speak with the spiritual conviction of former times. Perhaps it is not too much to say that no creed of our times is quite an adequate verbal instrument through which to convey the realities of the experience of God to modern youth. It would appear that some traditional religious conceptions actually block the way of the soul of youth in search of the experience of God.

Through the regular channels of the church doubtless a great deal is being done of the spiritual education of our youth. A few outstanding men in the pulpits are challenging youth with a new and constructive religious message. A new and modern approach to the study of the Bible is meeting the questions of many students on religious problems. The whole modern trend is likely to render an invaluable service to college students in their quest for truth. New inspiration has come to thousands of students through conferences that have frankly faced the whole gamut of the spiritual life of college men and women.

But perhaps something yet more fundamental and radical must still be done to meet the student mind of today. Our youth are the children of an age of science, and they are trained primarily in the scientific spirit and method. As Professor Whitehead says: "The mentality of an epoch springs from the view of the world which is, in fact, dominant in the educated sections of the communities in question." And the mentality of our epoch is scientific—and indeed has been dominated by scientific materialism. So, those who would seriously undertake the education of our youth must seek out anew in the spirit and patience of modern science, by the laboratory method, what the experience of God is, and what behavior of man will adjust his life to the divine life.

No claims of religion can be successful with modern youth which are not in accord with the facts of science. Religion and the experience of God will doubtless transcend science. But mere superstition, myths, legends, or archaic doctrines must be honestly forsaken when found untenable, no matter how hoary with age, before we shall have a vigorous experience of God in the hearts of youth.

Students will enter into enlarged spiritual insight through the deeper study of nature. New apprehensions of music and art will lend their contribution. There is no doubt that students will experiment and a richer and more autonomous ethical life will ensue. Humanitarian causes will command their enthusiasm. Thus in old ways and new they will seek and find expression to their highest moral and spiritual aspirations. Meantime the new mystic and the scientific pioneer and here and there a real prophet will appear and a new religious synthesis may be found that will satisfy the mystical, the ethical, and the social aspects of man as a religious being.

If, as we have seen, "the mentality of an epoch springs from the view of the world which is, in fact, dominant in the educated sections of the communities in question," then the *real* teacher of modern youth is our educational system. When we have all our youth in our educational institutions, then it is the school, possibly even more than the family or the church, that determines the mentality and the attitudes of youth. The university and the high school, whether they will or not, inevitably mold the life of modern youth, and their attitude to spiritual things whether it be for good or ill. Surely this is a great responsibility. It is beyond the bounds of this paper to discuss how they are fulfilling this unescapable mission. A recent study of the purpose of the college by Professor Leon B. Richardson states that the primary purpose of the higher institutions of learning is intellectual: "The ideal of the college becomes that of scholarship." And yet he confesses that "the development of intelligence uncontrolled by *moral purpose* becomes a danger rather than a help to the state."

The Commission on "The Objectives of Secondary Education," after naming as aims the evolution of the self, an appreciation of nature, and an appreciation of organized society, adds the final objective: "to promote the development of an appreciation of the force of law and of love that is operating universally." The report continues: "Man claims more than a knowledge of himself, of nature, and of organized society. He hungers and thirsts after righteousness. Knowing his own imperfections, he feels that somewhere there is perfection. The great universe calls to his spirit, and unless he ignorantly or wilfully closes his ears, *he hears the voice of God.* No question of theology or of ecclesiastical policy is involved here. The individual soul reaches out to orient itself in the universe and to find its place of labor and of rest. No partial view suffices. Only the view of the whole will make it possible to interpret the meanings of day by day experience. When this orientation takes place, life assumes poise, dignity, grandeur; otherwise its striving, its struggles, its achievements seem trivial and insignificant. *No greater task rests upon the secondary school than to help its pupils to find their God.* How this is to be done is the greatest of problems. Of one thing only we are sure. We cannot solve this problem by ignoring it." [1]

This report gives us a clue of what really constitutes the education of man. If the colleges and universities can conceive corresponding objectives, and in some measure attain them with modern youth, one of the greatest things that has ever happened in human history will have been achieved—education for the masses, education at once in efficiency, in the discovery and expression of native talent, and education in the experience of God.

[1] "The Department of Superintendence, Sixth Year Book," 1928.

AM I GETTING AN EDUCATION?

Sherwood Eddy

There are in the United States over a million college, university and normal students; by far the largest student body in the world.[1] How many of these are really getting an education? An undergraduate may find his time so filled with multiplied "activities" that he never stops to ask what is the purpose of his education, and whether or not he is achieving it.

If it is true that the individual student is investing some thousands of dollars, or an equivalent in work, and four or more of the most plastic and priceless years of his life in this process called education, will it not be well to deliberate long enough to ask himself whether he is receiving full value for his investment?[2]

We shall not do justice to all the facts if with cynical pessimism we can see no good in our present system of education, but only one vast "Goose Step" of slavish subservience. There is much to admire in our public school system with its broad and inclusive democracy. We are erecting the finest high school buildings and have incomparably the best material equipment for education of any country in the world. Some day we shall have a staff, a scholarship and a system of education worthy of such an equipment. In the matter of numbers we have achieved at least *quantity* in education, even if our youthful nation has not yet attained to a *quality* worthy of this bulk. In

[1] In 1926 there were 1,037,469 students in colleges, universities and normal schools. U. S. Statistical Survey of Education, 1926, p. 12.

[2] A brief calculation of the costs of an education might lead a student to think about results. Suppose I calculate what goes into my college course as follows:

Four years of time when I might be earning.........................
The labor of my parents in accumulating funds for fees and expenses....
Labor represented in endowments and state appropriations for my
    education ....
Costs to the community of an institution free of taxation; costs of
    museums, libraries, buildings, etc...................................
The Wesleyan Undergraduate Committee estimates that "each student in our American colleges today represents a direct or indirect cash investment of $25,000."

no other land are the highest attainments in university education so open to those who are poor, both men and women, in city and country. Some are recognizing that our colleges are living organisms, demanding constant growth. We find much encouraging experimentation in various institutions. Freshman Week to aid entering students in making adjustments, the orientation courses, courses in thinking, the comprehensive final examination in the major study, the tutorial system, sectioning on the basis of ability, the honors course, the growing concern for the student as an individual, the growing cooperation between faculty and students, the modernizing of tests, wider general reading, educational relations with the alumni, closer contact between the college and the real world—these are only a few of the encouraging signs observable in some institutions. [1]

Logically, we should first ask, "What is education; what are its aims?" The limits of space forbid a discussion of this question here. Perhaps most of us could agree that the purpose of education is the liberation of intelligence for the improvement of human life. As a provisional definition, having the advantage of being worked out by undergraduate students cooperating in reshaping the plan of education in their own institution, we may take the excellent statement of the students of Dartmouth, who maintain that the dual aim of education is the fullest possible development of the individual, and his adequate training for membership in society: "It is the purpose of the college to provide a selected group of men with a comprehensive background of information about the world and its problems, and to stimulate them to develop their capacity for rational thinking, philosophic understanding, creative imagination, and aesthetic sensitiveness, and to inspire them to use these developed powers in becoming leaders in service to society." [2]

---

[1] A record of the long, hard struggle for advance will be found in Cubberly's "History of Education in the United States."

[2] "Dartmouth Report on Undergraduate Education, Senior Committee," page 10. English educators have held that the main business of all education was to form in the mind of every person a single, wide interest, centered in a supreme purpose. Thomas Huxley thus defined a man of liberal education: "That man, I think, has had a liberal education who has been so trained in youth that his body is the ready servant of his will, and does with ease and pleasure all the work that, as a mechanism, it is capable of; whose intellect is a clear, cold, logic engine, with all its parts of equal strength, and in smooth working order; ready, like a steam engine, to be turned to any kind of work, and spin the gossamers as well as forge the anchors of the mind; whose mind is stored with a knowledge of the great and fundamental truths of Nature and of the laws of her operations; one who, no stunted ascetic, is full of life and fire, but whose passions are trained to come to heel by a vigorous will, the servant of a tender conscience; who has learned

The question of education is too large to grapple with all at once, for education is almost as comprehensive as life itself. Instead, somewhat arbitrarily, we shall break up the subject into several aspects, mindful in so doing that we are omitting many important elements and that the few we select overlap and are not wholly distinct. We recognize that to ask, "Am I getting an education?" puts the question too crudely and bluntly and is apt to be misleading. We do not regard education as a finished, short-time experience that one can "get." Education is, of course, not a body of information, or of external experience, but an increment of living to be ever enriched and expressed. Like freedom, it is not an external gift nor a finished possession but a life-long conquest.

As we ask ourselves whether in this sense we are getting an education, in our college or in life as a whole, let us consider the following aspects: (1) education as Thought, (2) education as Culture, (3) education as Life, (4) education as Growth, (5) education as Service, as the sharing of experience.

We shall ask ourselves under these headings the following questions:

(1) Am I learning to study and to think?

(2) Am I getting the knowledge that I need most? Am I learning to enjoy things that are most worth while? Am I acquiring aesthetic appreciation of the significant values of life?

(3) Am I living in the real world or in a corner apart? Am I learning to live, by living *now;* by acquiring some vital knowledge of the world and its real problems, by actually facing them and beginning to try to solve them now? Or am I evading or postponing life, playing about with its trifles in a thoughtless and unreal academic world?

(4) Am I progressing, standing still, or going backward? Am I growing in the various dimensions of life, on the physical and material plane, in intellectual breadth, in spiritual depth? Am I becoming the kind of person I want to become, and that I am capable of becoming, if I am to know life at its best?

---

to love all beauty, whether of Nature or of art, to hate all vileness, and to respect others as himself."

The late President Hyde of Bowdoin thus described the aims of a college education: "To be at home in all lands and ages, to count Nature a familiar acquaintance, and Art an intimate friend; to gain a standard for the appreciation of other men's work and the criticism of your own; to carry the keys of the world's library in your pocket, and feel its resources behind you in whatever task you undertake; to make hosts of friends among the men of your own age who are to be leaders in all walks of life; to lose yourself in generous enthusiasms and cooperate with others for common ends; to learn manners from students who are gentlemen, and form character under professors who are Christians, this is the offer of the College for the best four years of your life."

(5) How much am I worth, or going to be worth, to others? Am I so realizing education as the sharing of experience—a sharing between the older and younger generation; a sharing with teachers, writers, fellow students and fellow human beings, within and without academic walls—that in the spirit of service I may become, up to the measure of my ability, a possible leader, returning to society with interest what I am receiving in the gift of education?

If I am not measuring up to any of these aspects of education, wherein is the college failing and wherein am I myself falling short? If at any point I am not at present making good, how far can the institution or system of education be adapted or improved; and how far can I, whatever the system may be, win an education for myself, even as Abraham Lincoln did in the school of life? About me there is a world of men and books; there are instructors, students, classes, courses, activities; an institution, a community and a school of life. Some are getting an education and some are not; some will succeed and some will fail; the question for me at the moment is, "Am I getting an education?"

1. EDUCATION AS THOUGHT

Am I learning to study and to think?
Am I being taught How to think—or, What to think?

If the student is being taught *how* to think, the system of education is raising up potential leaders in a changing world. If he is being taught *what* to think, the process will perpetuate and petrify the evils of the *status quo*. It will seek to accommodate the future to the static past, instead of utilizing the imperfect past as resource for the developing future. It will not give vision or develop responsibility or initiative.

What is a college for, if it does not teach its students to think? Is not this the very heart of all education? If the college is failing in this central, vital matter of education as thought, what excuse has it to offer twenty-three centuries after Socrates? Have the great educators of the past lived in vain? Are we still under the spell of medieval classical authority; are we still merely relayers of information, handing down opinions that are to be swallowed whole, unchallenged and undigested? Dare we, like Socrates, provoke thought, release untrammeled the latent powers of the mind, and believe that it can find its way in a universe of reality?

Is education something primarily to be done by the teacher, or the student? Is it something to be pumped in, or to be drawn out? Is the student to be conceived as a hermetically sealed cistern to be filled with ideas, or as a well, fed from its own inner springs, released by the removal of encumbering débris? Is education to be handed down in artificial packages ready for use, or mined like ore in the sweat of one's brow? Is the student's mind a storehouse or barn to be filled merely with the harvest of other's thoughts, or a workshop where each builds his own machine that will run by its own power?

In a word, the first test of true education is what it does to the student. Does it teach him to be a passive and often even sullen recipient, or an eager and active creator? Body and mind we are made for action. No man will be greatly interested if he is made the unwilling receptacle of ideas not his own. Any normal student resents a system where he has to listen to, take notes upon, recite back by rote, cram up and write down in an examination, facts that are to him dull, opaque and uninteresting, because removed from his own thought, severed from life, and unrelated to creative activity.

The student must be on his guard at the outset, however, lest he seek an alibi in placing all the blame upon the faculty or the system of education. The faculty is heavily handicapped in dealing with students who come from Babbitt homes. The student will need to develop his critical powers in appraising his home training and the whole system of education, but he should first ask himself how far he is responsible and how far he is himself to blame if he is not getting an education.

More important than any external factor is the man himself. No faculty, no courses, no system, no library, can give a man an education if he has not the will to learn. It was not the four books in his log cabin and the six months of broken schooling that educated Abraham Lincoln. It was Lincoln himself. Ultimately no one other than yourself can educate you or rob you of an education. There is a library of good books at your hand, such a library as, for instance, Plato never possessed, for all his books could probably have been put into a wheelbarrow. Whatever the system, there lies within your reach an education, but only you can achieve it for yourself.

The student must press home the question: "Am I learning to think? If not, why not? How far is the present system calculated to stimulate independent thinking, and how far am I learning to think independently of the system?"

One of the first colleges to begin to break away from the traditional method of teaching was Dartmouth. President Hopkins invited a committee of twelve undergraduates to make a fearless and independent study of the current system of education and, with the faculty working independently, to suggest reforms or improvements. In their report to the president the students point out that their education fails because courses are taught without their ultimate end in view, and without sufficient effort to enlist the active interest of the student. The tacit assumption underlying such teaching is that the student is unwilling to work. And so he is, for the very system inevitably produces such students.

The Dartmouth student committee says: "The student can and will work of his own volition. The work that is done at Dartmouth in extra-curricular activities goes far to justify such a belief. The chief indictment against the present method of teaching is that the student is forced into a passive, rather than an active attitude. The criterion of passing is his ability to absorb, retain and regurgitate on the proper occasion about fifty per cent of the information the instructor sees fit to include in his course, together with the latter's supposedly authoritative commentary thereon." [1]

If students are spoon fed in college, they become in after life habitually uncritical of information offered to them. They form parasitic habits of thought, or rather lack of thought. The instructor tells the docile students what is right, what ideas and books may be considered authoritative. They form the habit of receiving truth upon authority and come in time to believe the account that best agrees with their own preconceptions and prejudices. The instructor frequently gives the material in just the form in which he wants it learned, and which will earn the highest grades. The successful student is not the thinker, but the mere stenographer so busy taking notes that there is no time or place for thought in the process. Independent or divergent thought is often not only not rewarded but penalized. The parrot, the sponge, the successful reciter and crammer, "gets by" in such a process. Unrelated facts are meaningless and soon forgotten. If the instructor proclaims the facts and ideas and the student merely memorizes them, neither is thinking nor encouraging thought. Neither is considering critically the foundations of belief nor developing the capacity for criticism.

The Dartmouth students continue: "Facts cannot find a place in the mind unrelated, uninterpreted, and unjudged. What we want from the faculty is not its interpretation, but exercise in interpreting for ourselves. . . . It is difficult to find a classroom where someone is not eternally trying to prove something, to club

[1] "Report on Undergraduate Education," Dartmouth, p. 21. President Hopkins wrote to the student committee: "The College is undertaking a complete survey, review and examination of its educational processes, in the hope that the way may be found to make these more influential and more effective."

the student into accepting someone else's judgment, be it in the form of a social creed, a literary opinion, or a scientific hypothesis. The faculty professes a desire to have the students think, but backs water usually when the thinking of any student begins to wreak havoc upon its own pet notions. . . . Fact and memory, without assimilation and application, are but learning without understanding, and knowledge without wisdom."

These students maintain that the lecture of the old type has degenerated into an attempt at mass education, and the classroom tends to become an arena for academic inquisitions and student bluffings. The daily quizzes and frequent hour examinations often fail miserably. The students now come to exist for the faculty instead of the faculty for the students. The faculty tend to degenerate into mere retailers of information. The emphasis is now upon the course at the expense of the individual. Taking and passing of courses becomes the criterion of attainment. The grade or mark, and hence the mechanics of attaining that mark, tend to usurp the place of the subject matter, and the symbol becomes the goal. The separation and often even hostility between teacher and student, and the present classroom, lecture-hall, final-exam system of education is the unhappy result.

In so far as our present system of education is merely teaching men unrelated facts and ideas instead of evoking thought, the evil results of the system are manifold and serious. Among these results may be mentioned the production of habitually docile minds incapable of thought and unused to initiative; a type of mass education that produces a standardized mediocrity of form, of fashion, of thought and action; the production of thought-less men, uninterested in the subjects and hostile to such a system, and colleges congested with an undesirable type of men who prove a drag upon those who really desire an education. By lowering the standard to the backward or indifferent men, the system discourages some of the better students and makes them lazy; it often inculcates standards of unreality in grading, marking, degrees, cramming, bluffing, "getting by," cribbing, cheating and other false adjustments to a faulty system.

President Wilkins, of Oberlin, writes: "The two traditional classroom methods are the lecture and the recitation. The ultimate reason why we have lecture method is because universities were founded before the invention of printing. The teaching profession, despite five centuries of printing, has not yet shaken off the medieval attitude; the teacher has not yet fully realized that many books on his subject, good books, books written possibly by even greater men than he, are readily accessible to his students. The presentation through lectures of large blocks of material which are in substance readily available in print is inexcusable.

Furthermore, the lecture process as a means of conveying information simply doesn't work with the typical modern undergraduate." [1]

After working among the students of more than a score of countries in Europe, Asia and America, with only one or two exceptions the writer does not recall finding any student body so docile in mind as that in the United States. In our country we are leading the world in almost every material and mechanical development. But as students we are not leading the world in thought, in initiative, nor in moral courage. [2] Our whole system of education does not tend to produce these characteristics, but rather their opposites; docility of mind, standardized custom, opinion and action. This is not education as thought.

The writer remembers when addressing the students at a certain state university, the most popular and intellectually awake professor said: "I am sorry that this morning you will have to address the seniors. You will find them unresponsive, intellectually dead, indifferent, or at times almost sullen in their hostility. We have made them so by our system of education. We have killed thought and interest in them. This afternoon, however, you will meet the freshmen and you will find them much more alert, open and interested. But they too will be intellectually dead four years from now."

Does the student care to pause and ask himself, "Am I learning to study and to think?" If his answer is negative, is he willing to take time to learn to think? Can he form the habit of questioning, of challenging, of criticising constructively, of taking nothing for granted? He will doubtless find that as the savages in the tropics are physically lazy, he is mentally lazy. But however slow, halting or inarticulate, can he not begin to form the

[1] "The Changing College," by E. H. Wilkins, p. 67.

[2] Dr. Herbert Gray, that discerning observer, after visiting the representative colleges of Britain and America writes thus of our educational system: "Your students are strangely docile in mind. Everywhere else in the world I find the rising generation in conscious and intense rebellion against the conventions and methods of life and thought which dominated their fathers, and which led the world to the present disaster. But young Americans are not rebelling. They are eagerly getting ready to go on in the old way. . . . I found among them little or none of that burning passion to discover a new way for mankind, which is the real hope of the world today. I was disappointed that they think so little about the great political issues and that their thinking is so conventional. I was dismayed at the number of them who seemed inclined to believe the papers and who will become later on the victims of mere fashion and the dupes of popular orators. . . . They seem to suffer from some strange paralysis of will. They often seem to lack the power to adopt a purpose and then follow it tenaciously and independently. I did not find the normal percentage of clear-cut personalities among them. Rugged and strong individualities are comparatively rare among them." *The Intercollegian,* October, 1923.

habit of letting no day pass, no lecture, no subject, no book without thought. Man, as distinguished from the rest of creation, is the "thinking animal," yet controlled or consecutive thought does not come naturally to him, but is an educational attainment. Where action is spontaneous or habitual it requires no thought, and we do not think unless we are forced to do so. Thought is provoked by the presence of an obstacle, a dilemma, a problem, a conflict that occasions a pain in the mind, or a fork in the road which involves a choice. Professor Crawford, in his "Technique of Study" makes a number of practical suggestions as to how a student may learn to think, such as the following: Define your problem; begin to think for yourself before consulting others; recall what you already know about the problem; obtain a good supply of fact and information that can be used as building material for thought; tentatively form hypotheses and arrange your material; plan systematically to cover the entire field you are investigating; analyse your problem and think on one aspect of it at a time; make use of writing as an aid to thought, to hold your mind on the issue and prevent it from wandering. Stimulate your thinking by talking with others, and use questions to direct your thought; use comparisons and contrasts; let your mind dwell upon the question in free association; give time a chance to incubate your ideas; clearly define your terms; face all the facts in the case and beware of substitutes, short cuts, or evasions; allow for your own personal equation, emotional factors and prejudices; beware of your own personal interest and of the power of suggestion which will prompt you to swallow whole without thinking; until you can criticize and verify your conclusions hold them as tentative; check them with the facts of actual life; finally summarize your results and state them in a nutshell in a few words.[1]

2. EDUCATION AS CULTURE

Am I getting the knowledge that I need most? Am I learning to enjoy things that are most worth while? Am I acquiring aesthetic appreciation of the significant values of life?

By culture I mean mental enrichment or the complete development of personality. In a word where I believe truth, goodness and beauty are ultimate realities, how far am I being "drawn out," as the root of the word education implies, to appreciate and respond to these realities? We naturally pity the cripple who cannot take part in the normal physical life of the college, the moron who has little or no capacity for knowledge, and the pervert

[1] "The Technique of Study," pp. 131, 154.

who has no sense of moral values. But what of the defective or crippled personality unawakened to the beauty and higher values of life? Our Puritan American tradition, busy with the conquest of a new continent, has far more developed its material resources and moral values than it has its aesthetic capacities.

Aristotle maintained that, "all men have by nature the desire to know." Probably they have until that desire is quenched by an artificial system of education or society that is contrary to human nature. If I am to become an educated man, whatever my special training or major subject may be, I shall desire to know something at least of the physical sciences, the social sciences and the arts. I shall want to know enough of nature, and of the world in which I am living, to understand the main processes upon which human life depends. I shall want to know how to live. I shall want to know enough of history, whether through formal courses or general reading, to understand what the human race has learned, to be able to judge current events in the light of the long perspective of the past; to be able to read the daily paper not merely for news, but to grasp the significance of present happenings as history in the making.

I shall want to know enough not only of nature but of human nature and human relations to live "the good life," rightly adjusted to my fellow man. If psychology is the "key subject in the modern intellectual advance," even if it is "still in the stage of groping infancy," I shall want to know what I can of myself, and of my fellow men, although psychology which teaches much of sensations and emotions often says little about the persons as an integer or the real values of life. My education should include the acquisition of essential knowledge, and training in the processes of how to acquire and use it. It should include not a superficial smattering of many unrelated things in an elective chaos, but related courses in general and special education.

To give a broad outlook, and to relate the disjointed fragmentary knowledge of other courses, many colleges are wisely providing a general orientation course. The object of such broad courses is to relate our scattered knowledge, to center, correlate and synthesize our information, connecting old and new, past and present, ideal and real. The student who seeks education as culture will recognize truth, goodness and beauty as ends in themselves, and true knowledge as worthy to be pursued for its own sake. But he will not regard education as consisting of the amassing of disjointed facts and unrelated information. Rather he will regard all facts as raw material for thought. They are not to be left like lumber in an unused attic, but used as building material which he as the architect of his own thinking is to shape to a purpose and build into life. Are the student's eyes being opened to beauty in nature, in art, in music, in literature, in the fine art of living? Or is he arrested on a jazz and movie level of life?

How many students are achieving education as culture, as the permanent enlargement and enrichment of life; how many demand, with the student committee of Dartmouth, that their college shall awaken creative imagination and aesthetic appreciation? "Our sensitiveness to form, color, and rhyme, our joy in art which is eternal, and our disgust at gaudiness which is cheap—those qualities the college must seek to bring to life. A man must be made to realize what the difference is between a life satisfied by colored comics, Coney Island, and radio jazz, and a life in which the appreciation of Shakespeare and Schubert thereby shares the emotion, and to some extent the greatness of the creators themselves. His aesthetic sensitiveness must be active not only in the enjoyment of art, which is external to him, but in the daily ordering of his own life so as to make it graceful, finished and fine. He must learn to detest a mere slumping through life; he must exercise that form of creative imagination which is possible to all in making living itself a thing of beauty." [1]

If an essential part of education is culture, am I acquiring a sense of values so that all through life I shall appreciate the significant rather than the trivial, choose superior rather than inferior enjoyments, place the enduring above the transitory, the social above the selfish, the beautiful above the base?

These interests may be found in the courses in arts and literature—or stifled there. More probably they will be created by the general tone and spirit of the college and its faculty. The college may be either rich or crude in culture. If the latter, I must seek no alibi, but all the more determine to find these values for myself.

Probably more important than any single course, perhaps for some more significant than all the courses combined, will be the use and appreciation of good books, and the formation of a habit of general reading that will last for a lifetime. The practice of discovery through independent reading is a chief means of culture. The student is fortunate if he is in an institution where at least one field may be covered by his private reading regarded as equivalent to a course. He is thrice fortunate if instead of being driven to certain assigned books in a compulsory course, he is able to form while in college the habit of good reading and of discriminating investigation for himself. Such a habit is in itself

[1] "Dartmouth Report on Undergraduate Education," p. 14. Culture, according to John Dewey, is "the capacity for constantly expanding in range and accuracy one's perception of meanings." "Democracy and Education," p. 145.

an education, for it opens up to him permanently a world of books and of thought.

The man whose education ends with Commencement, who closes his books with enthusiasm and never wants to open them again, is not an educated man. Rather he has been robbed of an education, whether through his own folly or by a faulty system. Apart from personal experience and contact with men, the normal means of education in later life is through books, especially current books and periodicals. If this habit of good reading is not formed in college it is usually not formed at all; certainly there is nothing in the world of modern business that tends to develop it. The college library and the college book store should play their part in this development.

How many of our undergraduates are forming for life this habit of good reading, and developing their aesthetic appreciation and enjoyment? How many of the alumni have these habits? Professor Angell estimates that the American undergraduate reads an average of only three books a year outside of his required work.[1] While the writer was journeying from one college to another, a college team entered the car and rode for some hours on the train. It was suggestive to hear their conversation and watch their habits. During that half day there was no word or act to indicate that any one of these men had ever been inside a college. They might have been professional players, or ignorant foreign immigrants, or dwellers in the slums, or beefy athletes paid to win games for the college, but neither then nor probably at any time during their lives, would most of them give evidence of intellectual or aesthetic tastes or appreciation of the higher values in life. Athletes they certainly were, but were they getting an education?

Visit an average fraternity house of undergraduates, or any college club in a great city. What is usually the drift of the conversation and what are the habits of voluntary reading? Professor Marks describes an average college club in a city: "Aren't any of them reading? you ask. One or two, perhaps, but probably none. Don't any of them go to the opera or to concerts? So

[1] In a mid-western university only twelve per cent of the students had read any literary or critical magazines before coming to college. In the University of Chicago it was found that the average individual does less than three hours of serious reading a week outside of required work. In the University of Michigan an average of only three books per undergraduate a year were read, more than half of which were for pure pleasure with no thought of gaining knowledge. "There is a lack of intellectual interest in undergraduate life and this is the product of the disorganization and the accompanying externalism of our times." Robert Cooley Angell, *The Campus*, pp. 21, 35, 65.

small a number that they are hardly worth counting. . . . Isn't there ever a discussion of anything worth discussing? I don't know; I can only report that I cannot remember ever having heard such a discussion. No dormitory or fraternity house in the land offers such a lethal intellectual atmosphere as a college club does. . . . There is no intellectual life in a college club; there is only the musty odor of death."

He concludes with an imaginary graduation scene after four years in a college which has encouraged no independent thinking in its students: "In presenting their degrees to many men, the college president might well say, 'With this sheepskin I am sealing your brain, such as it is . . . I hereby grant you permission to attain immediate mental death.' The graduating class will then rise and chant proudly, 'We who are about to die salute you'— and the ceremony will be over.

"When most seniors graduate, they put away for the last time their mortar boards and gowns and their intellectual life with them. Books become a thing of the past. A fiction magazine or two does for reading, an occasional musical show and the movies for entertainment, women for discussion. Business, bridge, bootleggers, radio, girls and automobiles: there is the complete list of the interests of the unmarried alumni. The list for the married alumni must be modified only slightly. For girls substitute family, and put more emphasis on radio." [1]

Allowing a little for the exaggeration of sarcasm in the above quotation, would it still not be pertinent to ask if any fair estimate could rate the majority of our undergraduates or graduates high in the scale of culture? Contrast with this picture of an American professor the description of education as culture in the words of Cardinal Newman: "A University training aims at raising the intellectual tone of society, at cultivating the public mind, at purifying the national taste, at supplying true principles to popular enthusiasm and fixed aims to popular aspiration, at giving enlargement and sobriety to the ideas of the age. . . . It is the education which teaches a man to see things as they are, to go right to the point, to disentangle a skein of thought. . . . He has the repose of mind which lives in itself, while it lives in the world, and which has resources for its happiness at home when it cannot go abroad." [2]

The writer's own experience in traveling among the colleges for many years has not led him to form a very favorable impression of the intellectual and aesthetic habits and tastes of our students. The following illustrations may be extreme, but they

[1] "Which Way Parnassus," Marks, pp. 108-111.
[2] "The Idea of a University," Newman, pp. 177, 178.

could be multiplied indefinitely, as almost every examining faculty member could testify.

In one of the two leading schools of journalism in America, the writer observed one of the students assigned to take notes of his address for the college daily, which was one of the best in the country. The writer had referred to the New Testament as "the book of John Huss" rediscovered by some of the students in Czechoslovakia since the war. This student reporter made the writer say that the problems of the world could be solved by a book just issued by a modern writer named John Husk!

After a lecture in a university in California, one of the students ingenuously asked the writer where he could buy the four books recommended in the lecture. As no books had been recommended, it took some time to discover that the student referred to the four gospels, Matthew, Mark, Luke and John, of which he had literally never heard. It may be as hard to believe this as the statement of Professor Phelps that one of his students had not the slightest notion of who Judas Iscariot was.

In an eastern college a student asked the writer for his signature in a book he had just purchased. Now this student had heard the words "autograph," "epitaph," and "epitome," but he was not quite clear as to their meaning, and one of them he could not even pronounce. With the accent on the first syllable, what he actually asked for was the writer's "epi-tome." Jim was a fine fellow. Our only question, however, is whether from the point of view of culture he was an educated man.

Are most of our college students getting a cultural education? Contrast with them the members of the Oxford and Cambridge debating teams who have been touring our country recently, often prepared to debate practically any question that might be chosen, if they were informed on the morning of their arrival, or ready intelligently to discuss any current issue. Granted that they were exceptional men; the same evidence of general culture will be found among students in a far wider circle in the English universities and over much of the continent of Europe than among the students of our country.

The acquiring of vital interests and aesthetic enjoyment in significant values and the habit of good reading will open up for any man a new dimension in life. It makes of life an enlarging, challenging, alluring adventure.

Viewed as culture, is my education doing this for me?

3. EDUCATION AS LIFE

Am I living in the real world or in a corner apart? Am I learning to live by living now; by acquiring vital knowledge of the world and of its real problems, and preparing to help solve them by actually facing them now?

Can education humanize the social order? Is education for life, or for some academic, artificial end divorced from it? There has always been a tendency for education, instead of furnishing leaders for society in a swiftly changing world, to drop out of the great midcurrents of life to its shallow and stagnant backwaters. There has been a tendency to mistake means for ends, to make of the college a little sheltered and cloistered privileged group, removed from the grim realities of birth, marriage, labor, suffering and death, for four years of artificial and irresponsible activities, very delightful, but far apart from vital contact with the real world.

At the recent Princeton Conference, Martyn Keeler, a Yale senior, said: "The college is an isolated community—passive, not living life at all. The whole atmosphere is that of the spectator's bench (not even a ringside seat), and we are not there primarily to be pleased by the performance. . . . The great bulk of the passive students are not interested *because they have never lived,* have never felt the pinch of need, and are making little real effort to do so." [1] College, with its grading, its honors, its pleasures, its achievements, seems to them to be the real world. Sometimes a subject is taught as if in a vacuum, whereas no subject exists by and for itself. The teacher should not teach, nor should the student learn, economics, sociology, or philosophy, each as an end in itself, but *living,* by the help of these subjects. Each is a tool of life; or else it is an impertinent obstruction. Each is a mountain peak or vantage ground gained by toil from which to view life as a whole.

In our tentative working definition, we held that education was for the dual aim of the fullest possible development of the individual and his adequate training for membership in society. The student comes from the community, and to it he will return. In a sense society supports him and has a right to expect something of him. If it is true that "the colleges in general are charging each student about half of what his or her education actually costs—that is, giving a half scholarship to every student, whether he needs it or not"; if, as we have said, it is true that each student represents a social investment of some $25,000, then surely society has a right to expect something from him. The college was created by society for social ends. It is not a cloistered hall where sons of privilege may learn gracefully to waste time and money

---

[1] "Report of Conference on Religion in the Colleges," Association Press, 1928, pp. 15, 18.

during four irresponsible years of a trifling playtime. What is the purpose of the college if it is not to train leaders for life? If the question is raised as to who should go to college, the answer of many educators would be: "Every potential leader—and no one else—a leader who will use his leadership for the good of society." [1]

Conceiving of education as life, once again we must ask the question, "What is college for?" Is it to educate a privileged group to enjoy life for themselves? Is it to train subservient leaders to preserve the *status quo* for the special privileges of a small minority possessing wealth and power? Or is it to raise up men as the builders of a new social order, offering larger opportunities for all? If students are being really educated for leadership, for service as members of society responsible to it, does it not then become axiomatic that *"no man is educated who is not socially awakened?"* No man is educated who has not learned vitally, at first hand, something of the nature, the problems, the conflicts of society. No man is educated who has had no practice in facing the actual problems of the real world, and honestly trying to solve them. If we are to humanize the social order we must first humanize the curriculum. Our reforms must be imbedded in our education. The college must be a part of real life and must face its real problems.

Does the college exist for building a bigger and better world? Or, is it to make bigger and better Babbitts, bigger and better stadiums, football teams and movies? Does the college exist merely as an adjunct of our defective social order to perpetuate its privileges and injustices? Is it to teach a *laissez-faire* economics and ethics, to sanctify mass selfishness and greed, to justify a hundred per cent nationalism, imperialism and capitalism?

John Dewey says that the subject matter of education consists primarily of the meanings which supply content to existing social life. The real world is facing certain crucial problems that are burning issues for the weal or woe of mankind—economic, racial, national and international problems. How far are the colleges facing them?

[1] President E. H. Wilkins, "The Changing College," pp. 74-81. President Wilkins lists the following qualities indicative of leadership: Seven moral qualities—ability to cooperate, moral cleanness, honesty, faith in knowledge, purposefulness, vision, social-mindedness; nine intellectual qualities—technical ability, power of expression, accuracy of observation, perseverance, power of concentration, sense of proportion, intellectual curiosity, power of initiative, ability to reason; four physical qualities—health of body, appearance, manner, attractiveness. How many of these do I possess? From the point of view of my value to society, am I a leader, socially am I earning my way, or am I a social parasite?

1. *There are vital economic problems unsolved.* What are the facts in our economic order? On the one hand, a relatively small group of privileged persons and families of wealth and power very largely control the industrial and political life of the nation. How far do they control the press? How far education? On the other hand we find masses of men in poverty, many of them crowded into slums which produce stunted lives and an alarming death rate. Many are unemployed, and no one acknowledges responsibility for them. At the moment of writing, the daily paper brings the news of an Indian Rajah spending millions upon himself, importing a European band for his private amusement, while the masses of his people are living in bitter poverty. The same paper mentions the fact of an American millionaire spending $25,000 on his six weeks' shooting in Scotland. During the hot summer months little children were dying in the slums of his city at three times the death rate for the well-to-do, and seven times their death rate from tuberculosis.

2. *There are challenging racial problems.* One privileged race is ruling some six-sevenths of the planet today; another race in our own country is segregated and subjected to indignities and injustices. Lynching is a national disgrace, yet we dare pass no adequate federal law against it. The Constitution guarantees the vote and equal privileges of citizenship to all, but sections of our country flagrantly deny them in practice.

3. *There are national problems* of political corruption, lawlessness and disorder, crime and graft, which are probably the by-products of our present social order of privilege and injustice.

4. *There are crucial international problems of war and peace,* of imperialism and industrialism. Are we to have an international chaos of sixty irresponsible, competing nations, or international law and cooperation, under which war shall be outlawed, and world problems faced and patiently solved by the organized functioning of an integrated world?

5. *There are unsolved problems in the relations between men and women,* a whole realm of sex problems neither solved nor even faced, but left too largely under a taboo of silence, with resulting ignorance and disastrous consequences for youth and age, for unmarried and married.[1]

How many colleges are freely, frankly and courageously facing the above problems, training future leaders to solve them by stimulating the students to begin to seek a solution now? The Dartmouth undergraduate committee asks: "Should the college continue to be bell-hop to the world in an age when the present criterion

---

[1] These are discussed at length in a separate pamphlet by the writer, "Sex and Youth."

of any venture is the commercial touchstone, 'Will it pay?' Or, on the contrary, has the college some more difficult function—to be the leader and not the meek errand boy of society, to set up ideals for the world?" [1]

The vital discussion of real problems raises, however, the whole question of academic freedom of thought and speech. Seen or unseen, realized or unrealized, there is in many institutions a silent, constant pressure brought to bear to prevent the fearless discussion of some of these problems. As between the trustees, the president, the faculty and the students, the first is the real governing body. The trustees are frequently officers in wealthy corporations, chosen because of their success in moneymaking; but they often know little of the problems of education. Special interests are always more concerned in preserving the privileges of the *status quo* than in building a new social order. They believe that the students should be given academic preparation for "a successful life," but not troubled with these "controversial questions." Every socially awakened college president, instructor, minister, or social worker, will feel the pressure of this money power if he speaks out on behalf of social justice. And the awakened student will feel it also. Fortunately—or unfortunately—not many in any of the above classes are sufficiently awakened socially so that they dare to speak out.

President Little, of the University of Michigan, says that one reason why religion lacks vitality in the colleges today is that students see that we are dodging the real issues: "When youth looks for a chance to come out and try new things, and to face modern conditions as they are, it finds on every hand obscurantism, and very skilful dodging of issues. Christ had to 'make' issues and pull weakness and hypocrisy out of their hiding place. The world is full of unchristian attitudes, and of efforts to obscure true issues." [2]

---

[1] "Report on Undergraduate Education," p. 16. In like manner the Wesleyan students ask for a one-year course in the most important problems of modern civilization, such as the following:

1. What is the sanest attitude we can take toward sex, marriage, and the family? 2. What steps can be taken for the eugenic improvement of the race? 3. How can future wars be prevented? 4. How can education be made more vital? 5. How far should the powers of government extend? 6. How can we insure business stability? 7. How can we insure fair play in industry and in the distribution of property? 8. How can we insure a steady advance in social and natural science? 9. What is the place of religion in society? "Wesleyan Undergraduate Committee Report," p. 18.

[2] "Princeton Conference on Religion in the Colleges," p. 26.

Professor Joseph Jastrow writes upon the subject "Who Runs the Universities?"[1] He complains that too largely politicians control the state universities, while business men exercise an unhealthy control over the colleges, and that neither are academically free. He thus quotes ex-President Schurman, of Cornell: "The president and trustees hold the reins of power and exercise complete control, while the professors are legally in the position of employees of the corporation. . . . The faculty is essentially the university; yet in the governing boards of American universities the faculty is without representation." President E. R. Craighead, in addressing the National Education Association, said: "College presidents . . . drive from the university all the independent and high-spirited professors. . . . They are the creatures, not the creators, of a system that threatens, unless reformed, to turn the temples of learning to educational gamblers and money changers." In Europe a university is a self-governing body. Too often in America, "control has left the campus and settled in the skyscraper." Dr. Jastrow concludes that "externalism in academic affairs is doomed because it speaks with authority and not with understanding. University or nation cannot flourish half slave and half free. The only way to emancipate the professor and save the universities is to make the academic career a worthy, authoritative profession. To that profession must be restored the directive control of the institutions of learning."

Professor Jastrow rightly objects to the unhealthy control of state universities by politicians, and of the endowed colleges by big business. But where do the students come in? In some countries an autocratic faculty control would be as much resented as a political or financial autocracy. In Russia, for instance, the curriculum of the institution is often determined by the representatives of the organized faculty and the organized student body acting jointly. And this joint body is equally concerned to eliminate not only subjects that have no place in the curriculum, but students who are not qualified effectively to study and members of the faculty not qualified effectively to teach. As in socialized business, labor, management and the public, all have a stake, so in the administration of the college we believe that students, faculty and the community all should have representation.

Professor Bode maintains that the most important thing about an educator is his social vision; that the question is not whether social vision affects educational practices, but whether in the long run anything else affects them. True education should mean world-

---

[1] *The Century*, April, 1928, p. 668. See also "The Story of the American College and Its Rulers," by J. E. Kirkpatrick; and "Academic Control," by Dr. Cattell.

building by the progressive remaking of our environment. The world will not be changed merely by increasing the amount of mass education. The Pharisees who compassed sea and land to make one convert ten times more a child of darkness than themselves did so by their effective process of education. Democratic society is concerned with future changes in the interest of progress, while governments are concerned chiefly with security and perpetuation; they are suspicious of novelty and change. Control of education whether by politics or industry tends inevitably toward stagnation and decay.[1]

The growing efforts of special interests to control public and private education for their own ends is of sinister import. The recent exposure of the efforts of the Electric Light and Power Companies to utilize the schools are deeply significant. Their instructions sent out to publicity agents for manufacturing public opinions combined "press and schools" as the agencies they wished to control. They spent millions of dollars in propaganda, including school text-books, to poison the minds of children and adults against public ownership.[2] To thus seek to corrupt the source of public opinion may be even more malevolent than our oil scandals or rotten politics. If we are to preserve democracy from the control of the money power and the exploitation of private monopolists, it behooves us to inquire again as to the freedom, the independence and creative quality of our education as life.

In this connection it may also be well to inquire how far democratic education, freedom of thought and speech are compatible with *compulsory* military training in our colleges. John Dewey and a growing number of leading educators maintain that military training in public educational institutions is "undemocratic, barbaric and wholly unwise." In how many colleges and universities where such training is compulsory, are the students allowed or encouraged freely to face these great social issues of our time?

---

[1] Boyd H. Bode, "Modern Educational Theories," pp. 209, 233, 235, 241.
[2] The disclosures at the investigation conducted by the Federal Trade Commission show that the power lobby organized to control the Congress of the United States had at its command during the last session of Congress over $400,000. The National Electric Light Association alone spent more than $250,000 for propaganda. Twenty-two state and regional bureaus spent some $700,000. Professors were paid for preparing textbooks for the common schools. A news service was controlled, reaching 14,000 daily and weekly papers. Vast sums were spent by this gigantic octopus to defeat the Boulder Canyon bill and the Muscle Shoals legislation. With over half the population of Europe and their educational systems already under dictatorships, is the money power finally to control government and education in America? See the report of the Federal Trade Commission, and the *New York Times,* October 28, 1928, p. 28; also *High Power Propaganda* by H. S. Raushenbush, New Republic Press, 421 W. 21st St., N. Y., price 25 cents.

Whatever the institution and its policies, is the reader facing these issues? Viewed as life, am I getting an education now?

4. EDUCATION AS GROWTH

Am I growing in the various dimensions of life, on the physical plane, in intellectual breadth, in spiritual depth? Am I becoming the kind of person that I want to become, and that I am capable of becoming, if I am to know life at its best?

1. *Physical growth.* A sound mind in a sound body has been an educational ideal from the days of ancient Greece. Athletics and college sports will doubtless always be a vital part of college education. And yet intercollegiate athletics are again on trial, no longer because of the danger of the games to the few who play on the teams, but because of their effect upon the vast majority of the students who do not. In the more thoughtful opinion of both educators and undergraduates, our often semi-commercialized and semi-professionalized college athletics have come under severe indictment. The report on Intercollegiate Football of the American Association of University Professors points out certain ways in which athletics help in the training of students in recreation and in creating a sense of common interest. Yet in their judgment, these are outweighed by the evils of the system. They hold that present-day college athletics create over-excitement, manifesting itself in the neglect of work, which is relegated to the position of a minor interest; that they interfere with the student's mental training; that they tend to the distortion in the student mind of the normal scale of values, in the worship of athletic success, sometimes coupled with scorn of intellectual distinction. They sometimes tend to create ideals of winning at any cost, which conflict with ideals of human service. They glorify publicity, financial display and a false standard of success. They intensify the drinking evil, the betting of the team followers, and certain forms of immorality. The demand for winning teams and highly paid successful coaches, leads often to the offer of improper financial inducements to players. Even if the game is played in good sportsmanship, as sometimes it is not, "the very presence of some of the players is evidence of a hidden and powerful and successful dishonesty, which is the antithesis of sportsmanship." [1]

The writer recalls two large denominational colleges that were once primarily an intellectual and moral force, turning out a good proportion of graduates of distinction and social leadership.

---

[1] "Bulletin of the Association of University Professors," Committee G, 1926, XII, 223; "The Changing College," p. 124.

Today they are "successful," with bigger and better teams and stadiums, an unsavory reputation and a cheapened and partially demoralized tone observable in the student body and among the younger alumni.

Various solutions have been suggested for our athletic problem such as "athletics for all," the one-year eligibility rule for varsity athletes, the two-year plan, the four-game plan, the class-team plan and the double-team plan advocated by President Little, of the University of Michigan, to increase the number of men engaged in athletics, and to do away with the costly football migration and its concomitant evils.

2. Intellectual breadth. As we have previously dealt with this point, we shall pause here only to ask, "Am I growing in my intellectual life?" Am I a candidate for truth? Have I a living mind? Am I acquiring breadth of sympathy and of interests and a wide and hospitable tolerance? American industry has flourished largely because it was flexible, willing to scrap machinery and methods that were obsolete. We are much more slow, however, to apply this same principle of flexibility to our individual intellectual growth, to our educational processes, to social usage, political organization and religious tradition. John Dewey says: "Our net conclusion is that life is development, and that developing, growing, is life. That means that the educational process is one of continual reorganizing, reconstructing, transforming. . . . Hence education means the enterprise of supplying the conditions which insure growth, or adequacy of life, irrespective of age."[1]

3. Spiritual depth. Professor Coe maintains that an educated man must have towards his fellows habitual attitudes such as honor, honesty, helpfulness, good-will, and coöperation. He must have loyalties to at least some of the important institutions of society, such as one's family, one's country, one's church. If he finds any inclusive meaning in life, he should have some apprehension of the divine; the ideally educated man will reverence God. He will have regard not only for God and man but for himself. President Hopkins believes that this generation of college men has no understanding of the imperative necessity of self-discipline.

True education teaches us to place a greater value upon quality than upon quantity in our habitual attitudes and estimates. If education is the continuous refashioning of life in accordance with ever nobler patterns, it will strike ever deeper into the inner sources of life. The uneducated man may be content to live haphazard, piecemeal, from hand to mouth, without thought or

[1] "Democracy and Education," pp. 59-61.

purpose or ideal. But the educated man cannot shape his life without vision or goal, without ever pausing to ask what is the purpose of life. If education is a coöperative enterprise to discover the deeper meanings of life, it cannot evade the quest of life's ultimate goal. A man may exist upon a purely animal or material plane, but as soon as he begins to integrate, to synthesize, to organize his life, to relate it to its source within, or to its great aims and objectives without, he has already passed over the threshold into the beginnings of philosophy or religion. The moment he seeks life's real values in truth, goodness and beauty, the moment he seeks some principle or cause to centralize or focus his life, he is beginning to enter upon education as growth, and education as character. If religion is "a man's most wholesome response to his total environment," if it includes in its bifocal emphasis vital relation to the Source of Life within, and ethical fellowship with his fellow men without, if it is an effort not only to see life steadily, but to *make* it whole religion will be found to be the very heart of education as growth in character. President H. A. Garfield, of Williams, writes: "In its broadest sense religion is the dynamic of education. Without it education is worse than ignorance, for without the guiding motive of religion, knowledge is a dangerous weapon and the educated mind a menace to society."

A conference on "Religion in the Colleges" was held at Princeton in 1928 attended by some two hundred leading educators. They maintained that religion is a vital element of racial experience, that if there is an antipathy to it in college chapels it is "not so much because of the irreligion of the students as because of the irreligion of the services themselves." [1] Members of the conference pointed out that there are in education two chief approaches to reality, the impersonal, scientific approach as in the physical sciences and mathematics, and also the personal appreciative approach as in the study of literature, music, the fine arts and religion. The student who would see life whole must cultivate not only the analytical but also the appreciative mind. Modern students will be appealed to not by the religion of the scribe, ever looking backward to the letter of the law, but by the religion of the prophet, the unending revelation of God to man and through man.

Complete education implies growth in character. Let us take the question of honor and of honesty. There are some colleges in

[1] The undergraduate committee of Wesleyan believes that "compulsory chapel is correlative with compulsory education—that if circumstances require one, we cannot hope to eliminate the other, at least in many of the smaller colleges. The ideal solution of the problem is to make the chapel exercises so worthwhile that attendance, compulsory or voluntary, is not a problem." "Wesleyan Undergraduate Committee Report," p. 26.

the country, which have an honor system that is successfully working, where they are, broadly speaking, prevailingly turning out men of honor. There are a few which are affording a good training of crafty politicians and crooked business men, where students are learning to evade, to "get by" and to avoid honest hard work. In such cases we believe that neither the college nor the individual student can shirk full responsibility. Some faculty members testify that "the amount of cheating in one form or another that goes on in our colleges is almost beyond belief," yet "the ideas concerning honor which the student adopts while he is in college determine largely what sort of man he will become." [1]

One recent graduate lists the following characteristics as tests of growth of an ideal personality:

1. Intellectual alertness and initiative.

2. A sense of honor and habits of honesty.

3. A sense of humor—taking your work seriously, but not yourself too seriously.

4. A rich appreciation of beauty, adventure, romance.

5. Love for humanity—a sense of oneness with all life.

6. A creative purpose in life *vs.* an imitative, routine mind.

7. Detachment from bondage to things—we live within, yet money can buy nothing within ourselves, but only the cheap externals of life.

8. Dedication of one's self to a worthy cause. "Three things a normal spirit craves; to live richly with his fellows; to understand himself and the universe, and how they fit together; a cause to serve."

How far is the college producing these marks of growth in the students? As growth and as character, am I getting an education?

5. EDUCATION AS SERVICE

How much am I worth, or going to be worth, to others? Am I realizing education as the sharing of experience?

Is there such sharing between faculty and students, between the older and younger generation? Does not any adequate conception of education and of life itself imply service and sharing? Life is not some isolated self-sufficient totality, but a continuous adjustment of internal relations to external relations, of organism to environment. We cannot compass education or life itself by any adequate definition satisfying to all. Education, like life, is a jewel of many facets, a growing organism adjusting itself to a changing environment. The old idea of education, both in theory and in

[1] "Which Way Parnassus," pp. 141, 152.

practice, was the imposition of truth by age upon youth, by teacher upon student, by authority upon its passive and obedient victim. But today we must regard education not as the imposition of truth but the promotion of growth. Mr. Dooley satirising the old idea says, "It makes no difference what you teach a boy, so long as he doesn't like it." Twenty-three centuries ago Plato recognized that "knowledge acquired under compulsion has no hold upon the mind." Awakened students strongly protest against the too-prevalent conception of some of the faculty that by compulsion you can stimulate in students a respect for learning as such. They protest against the results of this vicious circle, and deny that by professional activity you can compensate for student apathy, especially when the plan further entails a grading system and a police system to enforce it.

Does not true education imply the sharing of experience? If education is the continuous reconstruction of experience; if it is not to accommodate the future to a static past, but to utilize the past as resource for the developing future; if ideas are for the reorganization of environment and the improvement of life, surely education implies service and sharing. Dr. Dewey maintains that education is to develop men for the shared life of mankind. He says: "All education which develops power to share effectively in social life is moral." If education is the harmonious unfolding of all our faculties from within, a process by which the individual comes into constantly increasing possession of himself through participation in the achievements of the race, how else can he receive or give, how can he grow or truly live, save by sharing and serving?

Education then implies the sharing of experience not only between instructor and student, but, from the cradle to the grave, a mutual sharing between old and young, parent and child, the strong and the weak, professional and amateur, rich and poor, learned and ignorant. This implies education as vital, not mechanical; as a fellowship in the joint quest of truth, not a transfer of ready-made thoughts; as a continuous adjustment and advance, and not merely the rearrangement of prejudices and the perpetuation of a petrified system of error and injustice. This will involve a partnership and genuine participation between students, faculty, alumni and trustees. Unfortunately there is often a barrier between students and faculty. The students especially suffer from this, for it is chiefly through the faculty that they have any contact with the outside world. Unless there is mutual understanding between them, there arises an artificial wall of separation between instructors and students, and between the little artificial academic community and the real world without. The faculty may come to be regarded as the natural enemies of the students. The idea that students and faculty are working against each other is unfortunately all too common in many colleges. From the early inheritance of school days the teacher is sometimes thought to represent authority, compulsion, imposition and often punishment. During the past year the writer visited one institution where the tradition of the college had made an almost complete barrier between the students and the faculty. Any student found talking to an instructor was considered to be "boot-licking" or currying favor, and it was frowned upon both by faculty and students. The result was a kind of trench warfare between the two, the whole system instead of cooperation, service and sharing, was too largely imposition.

If we really believe in democracy should we not seek to embody it in our education? Autocratic training will not prepare men for future democratic leadership. Improvement of the present situation in the colleges will depend primarily upon faculty-student coöperation. Lecture and recitation must more largely give place to the joint quest for truth and to open discussion. Both faculty and students should be willing to learn from the progressive experiments which have recently advanced the technique of group-thinking.[1] Almost every institution that has appointed a joint faculty and student committee of equal members, or that has given a fair trial to the idea of education as the joint quest for truth, has been rewarded. The faculty members gain understanding of the student mind and conditions of student life. The students gain in friendly association with older men. Both may profit by coöperative effort in the joint quest for fact or truth.

Every fortunate student knows of at least one great teacher to whom he owes much of his education. Mark Hopkins on his log at Williams, Professor Garman at Amherst, William Rainey Harper at Yale and Chicago, are examples of men who have been loved for what they were and for the impress they made upon their students.

The writer recalls two faculty members; one was a beloved Socrates, held in affection by his students and by the alumni for forty years. Not all his students became prophets, or paragons, but numbers who completed his courses learned a hardy independence of thought, a love of good reading and a measure of responsibility for social service that makes this man's life a living monument. Contrast another teacher in the same subject, philosophy. He was a man of equal intellectual ability. Year after year his students have had their faith undercut; faith in man, or God, or service. The brilliant and ceaseless play of his

[1] Note the work of "The Inquiry," 129 E. 52d St., New York City, and that of M. P. Follett, E. C. Lindeman, A. D. Sheffield, Harrison Elliot, etc.

cynicism has undermined the character of many of them. In the estimation both of the majority of his students and of the administration his net influence has been almost wholly negative and destructive, not constructive nor creative. He has, apparently, never conceived of education, or of life itself, as service or as the sharing of experience.

One recalls two institutions. The first is not perfect in its processes of education; changes are doubtless needed in its faculty, and in some of its methods. But for many years it has left a stamp of character and service upon a large proportion of its students. During the last generation it has graduated and contributed to the leadership of our national life, ten bishops and some six hundred men to the ministry, over eleven hundred to Christian and social service, and a much larger number who have entered other callings and professions in the spirit of service. Like Edinburgh it has sent out its David Livingstones and Henry Drummonds, abroad and at home.

We recall a second institution. Doubtless there have been exceptions, but we have never met a graduate of that institution with any profound sense of obligation for service, with any strength of social passion, lifting up his voice or laying down his life for any cause involving the service of humanity. It is probably more than a coincidence that we have never discovered a single member of the faculty of that institution showing close touch with or deep concern for his students. The institution is heavily endowed; the faculty members are well paid professional teachers; the students are a motley crowd, unorganized, unrelated to education as service and as the sharing of experience. The idea of the joint quest of truth by faculty and students would be far removed from the conceptions of either.

We think of two students whom we might contrast, recent graduates of the same western college. Both have gone through essentially the same required courses, passed almost the same examinations and have taken the same degree. But one has begun to achieve and is ever continuing to achieve an education, and the other has not. The first man learned to think while in college. Independence of thought, sound judgment, thorough mental processes characterize his work. If we test his education as knowledge, his courses did not result in a mere smattering of unrelated subjects, but he has built up during his college course and since, a sound body of information and a solid foundation which will carry as great a superstructure as he can build. He is an authority upon one subject and has a wide range of information upon many. Tested as culture, his education is not as rich as some, but many of his early limitations have been removed and he has tastes and interests that would mark him anywhere as an educated man. He has formed the life habit of good reading. Above all he has entered into education as life. He has seriously come to grips with the outstanding social problems of the day and in several fields he has made a notable and courageous contribution. If we test his education by the criterion of character, he is known to all his friends as a growing man. He has indisputably a living mind. You cannot always account for him. He is not static or stationary but has always forged a little ahead, so that others wonder just how he accomplished the last task, or how he did the unexpected thing. If we conceive of education as service or as the sharing of experience, he has entered into the rich treasures of many minds—among his teachers, his friends, his books, classic and contemporary. And what he receives he gives back in good measure, sharing to the full with his fellow men.

Let us contrast with him the second student. He was a member of the same college and joined a good fraternity. If we view education as thought, he has probably never in his life spent an hour in meditation nor in anything that could be called consecutive thought. He is indeed quite incapable of it, for he allowed his teachers to do his thinking for him. His painful experiences of examinations, note-books and text-books have left no enduring foundation of education as knowledge. Books he never learned to love in college or since. Of education as culture he knows little. He knows how to shake hands heartily with a fraternity brother or a fellow Rotarian. He enjoys a good movie. His tastes are still on the jazz level, now somewhat slowed down from the din of the fraternity house to the monotony of his home and its radio. Education as life is to him unknown. He is now in the busy scramble of a bread and butter existence for the possession of material things. He confronts the problems of the social order merely with his old prejudices, scarcely even rearranged. Of education as continuous growth, or as service in the sharing of experience he knows almost nothing. He has not consciously failed to achieve any goal or spiritual ideal because he never had such.

Here are two men who represent two types familiar in all our colleges. The life of the first is creative, the second merely acquisitive. The one is living a life, the other is just making a living. Judged by almost any standard the first is an educated man, the second is not. Here are two types of men in college and in the great school of life itself. To which class do I belong?

In conclusion, to repeat the question with which we began, *Am I getting an education?*—Education as thought, as culture, as life, as growth, as service in the sharing of experience?

EXCERPTS FROM WHAT AILS OUR YOUTH [1]

George A. Coe

What has happened to our young people? The faults that everybody notices are easily summarized: Craze for excitement; immersion in the external and the superficial; lack of reverence and of respect; disregard for reasonable restraints in conduct and for reasonable reticence in speech; conformity to mass sentiment—"going with the crowd"; lack of individuality; living merely in the present, and general purposelessness. Even among college students, as we are told on all hands, there is dearth of intellectual interests. Dawdling is general, and the most absorbing occupations are recreations and athletics. Merely to bemoan these things is bootless. We shall discover that the young are reacting in natural ways to conditions for which we, their elders, are responsible, if anybody is.

Our industrial civilization itself is ailing, and it communicates its ailment to the young people. The young people of today are helplessly immersed in this industrial system, which is not organized in the interest of young life and its development, but of income, profits and spending. The occupations of men impoverish the spirits of men, and then with ready money invite them to seek refreshment in things that can be bought rather than in things that can be had only by achieving them. This is true, on the whole, of academically privileged youth. Our youth need stimulus to the critical evaluation of property, profits and power over men. On the whole, then, education itself is reproducing in youths, instead of correcting, the moral confusion that prevails in adult life.

What significance for life ought the triumphs of modern science to have? Are any of our fellows being hurt, repressed, or neglected because we employ the sciences in our occupations? Unless in education we open questions like these, we must expect our young people to look upon the resources of the world partly as playthings, partly as instruments for unhumanized economic purposes.

[1] Quoted with the kind permission of Charles Scribner's Sons, Publishers, New York. The quotations are not continuous.

What ails education? A rapidly changing world, and slowly changing schools and colleges—this is the fact with which we have to reckon. Why is it that the colleges do not make *education for the vocation of living* their supreme purpose and test? What has conventionalized and mechanized them? What has dulled the spiritual apprehension of teachers and administrators?

The development of fresh life-purposes through education is hindered by the still prevalent view that teaching is something done by the teacher to the student. Hence the essence of most examinations could be phrased as: "What is this that the professor has thrown at you?" From the student's point of view the question might be worded. "What has hit me?" The A's and the Phi Beta Kappa keys go to the men and women who give the fullest descriptions of the professor's missiles.

The teacher merely "puts over" his own purpose. He selects *for* his students; he does not educate them to select for themselves, or to form purposes in ever broader and broader circles. The lack of experience in making important judgments and choices explains the conventionality of some students and the anchorless drifting of others.

Here is one factor in the spiritual dulness, or at least conventionality, that generally characterizes the administration of the colleges. How different would they be, and how different would be the place of both student and teacher in the social structure, if teaching were understood to be, first and foremost, the stimulation of students to a critical examination of the values of our civilization!

Education for the vocation of living has been hindered, likewise, by the manner in which the necessity for specialization in teaching has been handled. The department of physics teaches physics, not living by the help of physics, nor the possible improvement of life by physics, nor the evils that accompany the present applications of mechanical laws in industry. Whatever outlook there is in the department of physics toward vocation concerns simply the control of matter, as in engineering, without reference to the human interests.

What would happen if the whole of the high school and college curriculum were to be organized around such questions as these: What shall I need to do, and therefore to know, as a voter, a taxpayer, a married person, a parent, a member of a church, a member of the community; especially, what are the unsolved problems of life and society, and what decisions may I be called upon to make? Why is there so much unhappiness? Why don't we get rid of ancient, recognized evils?

Why should we be puzzled at all by the lack of intellectual interest in the colleges? It is the natural result of dissecting knowledge into dead specimens instead of acquiring and using it for the living purposes of men now living. And why should the immersion of students in athletics and recreations, college publications, dramatics, and what not, be a mystery to us? These young persons have an urge to do things that employ their powers of initiative, judgment and management.

A critical approach to the values of modern life has been hindered by the financial dependence of the colleges and universities. The system of administration gravitates toward the level of those who fill the purse. One does not need to look for any specific purpose to make our colleges adjuncts of our defective economic order. For the most part there will be depression rather than suppression—that is, such mechanization of the professorial mind that one does not even desire to utter judgments upon the major issues of life. Why are our youth ailing? Partly because the spirit of our ailing industrial order has infected our colleges and universities.

When is a youth well-educated? A good education is education for good living. Life is for something, and education is for life. What an absurdity it would be to certify as well-educated a youth who never has been socially awakened—well-educated, yet negligible as far as social well-being and social progress are concerned! To the extent to which current education does not contribute to a social awakening, we must trace the social heedlessness of our youth to the schools and colleges.

If we were challenged to describe the really educated man, what items certainly would be included in our answer?

1. An educated man is one who is trained to use the tools of human intercourse with readiness, precision and accuracy. We mean, especially, language and the rudiments of number.

2. An educated man must be able to study and to think without guidance from others. He must be—to some extent—a thinker, not a mere imitator.

3. An educated man must have sufficient knowledge of nature to understand the main processes upon which human life and happiness depend.

4. An educated man knows enough of history to enable him to understand the main achievements of man.

5. An educated man is acquainted with the major resources for intellectual and aesthetic enjoyment. He knows nature, literature, music and the other arts sufficiently to choose superior to inferior enjoyments.

6. An educated man is marked by his interests as well as by his trained abilities. His attention is habitually attracted by significant rather than trivial objects, events, pursuits and enjoyments.

7. An educated man must have not only this general culture but

also training for a specific occupation. Focalized activity that is directed toward some sort of efficiency has to be included.

8. An educated man must have toward his fellows the habitual attitudes that are commonly called ethical—such attitudes as honor and honesty, helpfulness and good-will and coöperation.

9. An educated man must have loyalties to at least some of the important organizations and institutions of society, such as one's family, one's country, one's church.

10. If there is an inclusive meaning in life, the sort of education that I have been outlining should include some apprehension of, and feeling for, the divine; the ideally educated man will reverence God, and know how to worship.

A just ideal of education as a whole will make two assumptions in addition to those already formulated, namely, that this is and ought to be a changing social world, and that the prime function of educated men and women is to make appropriate social changes.

Education should preserve and cultivate, not neglect or suppress, the natural variability of youth. In the natural variability of youth, the possibility of a progressive civilization chiefly lies. To cultivate the natural variability of youth four things are necessary.

1. A focalized and concrete ethical outlook. A focalized and concrete ethical outlook cannot be given by a professor to a student. It must be developed as the student's own habit of mind.

2. Knowledge of the structure, the processes, and the strains and conflicts of present society.

3. Vital knowledge is, of course, something more than a mere information as to facts. A youth is not well-educated until he has had practice in the critical valuation of the institutions and the ways of the society of which he is a part.

4. This criticized practice in individual variation will fully ripen only when it includes experience in making social changes as well as devising them. How can we possibly count as well-educated any man or woman who never has taken any significant part in the final determination of the social conditions and the educational conditions under which he or she lives? A baby in arms is not a fitting crest for a college or a high school. The idea that one begins life after one gets one's education is not only absurd, it is socially destructive.